The Steam-Powered Automobile

An Answer to Air Pollution

The Steam-Powered Automobile

An Answer to Air Pollution

Andrew Jamison

Indiana University Press

Bloomington
London

To
Barbara Jamison and
Saunders Jamison

Contents

One   The Poisoned Air   3

Two   Detroit's Reaction   14

Three   The Steam Car Historically   35

Four   The Steam Car Today   52

Five   The Steam People   69

Six   Lear   84

Seven   California's Activity   98

Eight   The Role of the Federal Government   114

Nine   The Other Alternatives   129

Ten   Some Conclusions   142

Notes   153

Index   163

Acknowledgments

I would like to thank my editors at the news department of *Science*—Dan Greenberg, who worked with me on my first article on steam cars in June 1968, and John Walsh, who saw me through to the end; Hunter Larus and Bryce Nelson of *Science*, who contributed assistance far beyond the call of duty; Karsten Vieg, formerly of the California State Assembly Office of Research, who opened his voluminous files (and his spare bedroom) for my use; Dr. Robert Ayres of International Research and Technology, who read the manuscript and made very helpful suggestions; Bruce Collier, Tom Roberts, and Mona Sarfaty of Harvard; and the directors of Indiana University Press, who first saw the need and the potential for this book on steam cars.

I would also like to thank all those who granted me personal interviews. Quotations not cited in references are taken from these interviews or from the hearings on steam-powered automobiles held in May 1968 before the Senate Commerce Committee and the subcommittee on air and water pollution of the Public Works Committee.

The Steam-Powered Automobile

An Answer to Air Pollution

Chapter One

The Poisoned Air

The air in this country is not getting any cleaner. While money and time are spent studying, analyzing, and talking about the dangers of polluted air, the situation stays much the same, or gets a little worse. We have grown accustomed to dirty air, much as we have come to accept stagnant lakes and rivers, poor public services, and crowds and traffic everywhere. Polluted air, we have too easily assumed, is one of the prices of affluence, one of the necessary evils of industrialization.

The evidence continues to pile up, however, that polluted air carries a cost that we are not able to bear. We cannot afford to have dirty air; it is too dangerous. Report after report links high levels of air pollution to shortened lives, to increased incidence of lung and heart disease, to crop damage, and to deterioration of resources. Air pollution is a major health hazard not confined to Los Angeles, New York City, or big cities in general. Polluted air has spread across the American landscape like a plague. And like the carriers of a plague, the major carrier of air pollution—the automobile—must be identified and made harmless.

We have reached the point that every city, large or small, with a factory or two and a large number of automobiles is sure to have a haze of filth in the sky. There is a pollution problem in Denver, Colorado, in Butte, Montana, in Phoenix, Arizona, and in Grand Rapids, Michigan. No area is immune.

Control of stationary sources of pollution—factories, incinerators, power plants and the like—although important, touches less than half the problem. One estimate breaks down the sources of air pollution in this way: 2.6 per cent from refuse disposal, 6.3 per cent from space heating, 12.5 per cent from electricity generation, 18.7 per cent from manufacturing—and 59.9 per cent from motor vehicles.[1] Clearly, the internal combustion engine that drives all but a handful of today's motor vehicles is the major uncontrolled source of air pollution, and its control or replacement will be necessary before the levels of contamination will be significantly lowered.

The Los Angeles experience is a case in point. Since the mid-1950s, the Los Angeles Air Pollution Control District (APCD) has vigorously battled stationary sources of pollution. Under the leadership of S. Smith Griswold and later Louis J. Fuller, it has imposed strict controls on industrial polluters, requiring the use of low-polluting fuels by industry and private individuals, and banning commercial and domestic incinerators. The stationary sources have been so controlled that 90 per cent of the air pollution in Los Angeles is now contributed by automobiles. But since the number of vehicles keeps increasing, the pollution has not actually decreased—it has "more or less stabilized," according to one official.[2] And it has stabilized at a high and dangerous level.

Los Angeles is particularly unfortunate in its geographical location and its climatic conditions. The city is surrounded by mountains on three sides and, during about three-fourths of the year, experiences temperature inversions which keep the pollutants hovering over the area. Under normal conditions, the air gets gradually colder with altitude so that the warmer air from below is able to rise. Since polluted air is usually heated, it is ordinarily dispersed by this normal rise and the movement of air masses.

During a temperature inversion, however, the upper layers of air are warmer than the ground air and the pollutants must accumulate near their places of origin. Once the inversion occurs, it often perpetuates itself. That is, the pollutants—kept from rising by the lid of warm air—will form a foggy haze above the city that prevents the ground air from warming while the haze itself absorbs more heat from the sun, thus strengthening the inversion.

Los Angeles during its dry season has one of the most persistent inversions on earth, but the phenomenon can and will happen anywhere.[3] And whenever an inversion combines with a large amount of pollution, disasters can occur. Some of the worst have taken place in areas that do not have frequent temperature inversions. At such times, air pollution has killed in large numbers.

In October 1948, a temperature inversion hit Donora,

Pennsylvania, and soon a thick haze from the town's steel mills covered the city. For four days, the visibility in Donora was limited to two or three feet. Almost half of the town's 14,000 residents became ill, and twenty died. "People began to have a lot of respiratory diseases, actually were choking, and we didn't know why," said one Donora doctor. "You'd make a house call and before you could leave there would be several people at your car, grabbing you to see somebody at their house."[4] Since then, the town's mills have closed and the population has dwindled. Donora's mayor sees ominous parallels to his town's disaster. "I've been to Los Angeles several times," he said in a 1967 radio broadcast, "and what I see in Los Angeles almost every time I go there is what we had in Donora in this particular episode."[5] Although the deaths in Donora were caused mainly by non-automotive pollutants, especially oxides of sulfur, and Los Angeles' smog is caused largely by motor cars, the mayor's point is valid. Pollution is dangerous and in a temperature inversion can be deadly.

Three similar disasters have struck New York City in the past twenty years. As in Donora, temperature inversions left the city smothered in contaminants from its factories, incinerators, and automobiles. The pollution was not so visible as in Donora but it was just as deadly. Dr. Leonard Greenburg, New York's first Commissioner of Air Pollution Control, has calculated that the disasters killed over 700 people. From his study of hospital records —the deadly results of the pollution had not been realized at the time—Greenburg found that in one two-week period in November 1953, there were 220 deaths for which there was no explanation other than air pollution. Ten years later, 400 people were killed in a prolonged attack. As recently as 1966—over the Thanksgiving

weekend, when the traffic levels are among the highest of the year—168 individuals died from air pollution.[6]
In order to avert such tragedies in the future, New York City has instituted emergency detection and control procedures. Like Los Angeles, it has sought to control stationary sources of air pollution. But the number of automobiles on the streets of New York keeps increasing. Recent controversy over the expected pollution levels from a new expressway planned for the lower end of the city kept construction "under discussion" for years and the project finally was canceled. In June 1969, Mayor Lindsay warned that automobiles might have to be banned from the city altogether. "Can we continue to permit millions of automobiles, powered by internal combustion engines, to swarm through city streets . . . spewing more and more deadly chemicals in our air?" he asked.[7] Several times in the past few years, New York City and Los Angeles have been struck by smog alerts. The cities have been brought to a standstill and people with respiratory diseases and heart ailments advised to stay indoors. Other cities are also periodically paralyzed by air pollution.

The air pollution problem is not merely an American dilemma, although it is most acute in this country. England, Japan, the Soviet Union, and Germany also have dirty air, varying in intensity with the degree of industrialization and the number of motor vehicles.

The worst pollution disaster of all occurred in London in December 1952, when a four-day inversion layer left an estimated 4,000 more people dead than would normally have died. It has been noted that in that episode, unlike all the others that have been reported, the death rate increased in every age group by a similar percentage. In most other disasters, elderly people and infants have been the usual victims, but in London's 1952 pea-soup smog all age groups were hit indiscriminately. This suggests that the more intense the smog, the more overwhelming the danger to every individual.

If heavy air pollution can kill so quickly, and on such a large scale, then how can we be sure that relatively mild levels of it are not killing us slowly? In truth, we seem to be involved in a permanent air pollution disaster, with no level really safe, no exposure really healthy. The goal should be to get the air as clean as possible because if we don't, everyone—the industrialist who spews contaminants from his factory, the auto maker who builds vehicles which are the major source of pollution in this country, the individual who heats his home and drives his car—is in some degree responsible for the deaths of many of his fellow citizens, and perhaps even of himself.

At the present time, we do not know how much air pollution we can live with—or in. Calling any level safe involves a risk—a risk with our lives. A recent Senate report, prepared for the Subcommittee on Air and Water Pollution of the Public Works Committee, says that the attainment of better air quality "assumes that where a risk exists, all methods of control that are technically feasible and economically reasonable should be employed to minimize the risk."[8] It seems clear at the present time that we are not following this dictum.

There is much statistical evidence that links high levels of air pollution with higher incidence of heart and lung diseases. There has been a good deal of experimentation on animals to determine what levels are dangerous to them, but experimentation on humans has been limited. We know fairly well at what level smog in the air irritates the eyes, but at what levels do contaminants make breathing difficult? At what levels do contaminants begin to break down resistance to disease? At what levels do contaminants start to damage lungs (a process, like the others mentioned here, that may take many years)? Much more investigation will be necessary before these questions are answered precisely, but the evidence we do have indicates definitely that air pollution is a hazard to health.

Motor vehicles emit carbon monoxide, hydrocarbons (compounds of hydrogen and carbon), oxides of nitrogen, and smaller amounts of lead, oxides of sulfur, and particulate matter. The main contributions from stationary sources are large amounts of sulfur oxides. All these pollutants can kill, some by themselves and some in reaction with sunlight or other pollutants. Various oxidants (of which ozone is the most common) are produced by the photochemical reaction of certain hydrocarbons and oxides of nitrogen with sunlight. This reaction brings about visible smog, the haze to be seen on most days in downtown Los Angeles.[9]

Carbon monoxide, nitrogen dioxide (one of the oxides of nitrogen), and lead all are toxic to humans. Certain oxidants have been found to harm the lungs and multiply the incidence and intensity of emphysema, which is the most rapidly increasing cause of death in this country. At high enough concentrations, these pollutants can kill. Among the most deadly is carbon monoxide, some 66 million tons of which are emitted annually from motor vehicles.

Carbon monoxide, an invisible, odorless gas, interferes with the body's use of oxygen. Red blood cells ordinarily combine with oxygen in the lungs and carry it to the rest of the body. Carbon monoxide, however, combines with the red blood cells much more easily than does oxygen, so that when it is present, it and not the vital oxygen is circulated. Slight amounts of carbon monoxide in the

blood produce no perceptible effects, but it is unclear
whether carbon monoxide has a cumulative effect on the
human system. Such effects have been observed in animals, and have led some scientists to suspect that continuous exposure to low levels of carbon monoxide may be
very serious indeed for humans. Such exposure, two re-
searchers have written, "may have a role in the development of human heart disease."[10]

At certain levels—when carbon monoxide is at a concentration of 30 parts per million (ppm) for several
hours—the gas can bring about impairment of vision,
and at slightly higher levels, it can affect breathing. As
with almost all pollutants, the effects of carbon monoxide
pollution will be greater for smokers than nonsmokers
and will also be greater at higher altitudes where the
oxygen pressure is decreased. Carbon monoxide is also
more dangerous for people already suffering from respiratory diseases or from ailments that affect the circulation
of blood to the tissues.

Recent experiments have shown that carbon monoxide
may affect sensory awareness in the brain. Animals exposed to 50 ppm of carbon monoxide for ninety minutes
on each of four days in succession have been found to
have slower reactions than normal. In fact, the effects on
animals of carbon monoxide exposure is very similar to
those observed from pentobarbital, which has been
found to depress the visual awareness of animals.

Human beings exposed to the same concentration for
just forty-five minutes—exposure similar to that on many
busy city streets during rush hour—were unable to gauge
time intervals as well as an unexposed group. "We can
only speculate," a researcher has written of this experiment, "upon the importance to driving performance of
the capacity to estimate a one-second interval to within

an eighth of a second."[11] It could be disastrous, and probably has been an untold number of times.[12]

Recent experiments indicate that other pollutants are hazardous to health, as well. It has been shown, for example, that ozone and nitrogen dioxide can induce cancer in animals and damage the lungs. These results have been obtained at concentrations ordinarily encountered in city traffic. Emphysema has been linked to air pollution as well as to smoking. Pneumonia has been shown to occur with greater frequency in animals that have been exposed to various pollutants than in unexposed animals. Another study, by the U. S. Public Health Service, found that a high school cross-country team did consistently worse on polluted days. The runners were affected by the levels of oxidants in the air, and very low levels at that. One part per hundred million units of air, which is fairly clear air, was found to affect the performance of the runners. "If a smoggy day makes a young athlete just a little more tired," one analyst commented, "an older man with cardiac trouble had better not run for his bus on such a day, or attempt any other exertion that might tax his injured heart."[13]

Other research findings are just as ominous. Animals that have been exposed to pollutants have been found to be more susceptible to bacteria. In one experiment, mice were exposed to smog and later were found to be less fertile than unexposed mice. They were also found to be more susceptible to streptococcus and pneumonia organisms, as well as to various viruses and germs that cause heart and lung diseases. Such experimental findings cannot directly be applied to humans, but they suggest that air pollution is at least partly responsible for susceptibility to disease. Incidence of lung cancer, for instance, has increased substantially in recent years, and the increase has been noted in nonsmokers as well as in smokers. It may be significant that the increase has been largest in urban areas. Working alone or with other factors such as smoking, previous respiratory disease, or more frequent exposure to diseased individuals, air pollution is undoubtedly one of the major hazards to health faced by the city dweller. Urban living may be chopping time off his life, perhaps as much as several years.

Because of its well-known toxic effects, lead is used cautiously in home and industry. Particular care is taken to keep paint with lead pigment away from children. There is as yet, however, no standard limiting the amount of lead that automobile exhausts can pour into the air of this country. In a report released in late 1967, a Department of Commerce panel recommended that the government impose a restriction on lead emissions so that there would be no "further increase in the total quantity of lead emitted to the atmosphere."[14] In addition to indicating that there may be serious unhealthy effects caused by lead emissions from cars, the panel also pointed out that lead in gasoline seems to increase the emissions of hydrocarbons.

The present absence or slackness of standards for controlling air pollution is distressing. The gaps in our knowledge offer no real excuse for lack of action. As a former researcher, now a research administrator, has put it, "The British reduced cholera and typhoid in the nineteenth century before they knew bacteria existed, and we may have to regulate our air supply before we have complete knowledge about air pollution. The methods we have for detecting excess deaths are so crude that there has to be a pretty big excess for us to realize that it's there at all. What we *do* know is that people get killed by air pollution, and I don't see any excuse for there being enough air pollution to kill people."[15]

If the threat of serious disease is not sufficiently moving, air pollution hits severely in a different area—the pocketbook. The Public Health Service has estimated that pollution costs the country some $12 billion a year, and some officials put the cost even higher. Many smog authorities, however, are wary of making any estimate of pollution's financial costs. "It is not a linear relationship," says one official, "between air control and benefit derived, and we shouldn't have to work on that kind of a basis. It's nice to have the philosophy that it's just better to have clean air than dirty air."[16] We are now probably past that stage. We are at the point where it is not only better to have clean air, it is essential.

Pollution's cost is not limited to its effects on human beings; it has long been known to be harmful to plants. One air pollution authority has estimated that smog annually damages crops and flowers and trees worth $250 million in California alone.[17] Ozone is probably most responsible. Since the automobile first began to invade southern California in earnest after World War II, the area's flower industry has wilted. Formerly a $14 million a year business, flower growers in the Los Angeles–San Diego area are now down to about $3–4 million a year. It has become almost impossible to raise flowers in southern California, and crops throughout the state—as well as in twenty-two other states—have been increasingly hurt.

It seems apparent, then, that dirty air is a luxury we cannot afford. We are killing ourselves, as one doctor has put it, by our own effluents. We are playing with our environment in ways that we do not yet understand. The smoke from industrial plants and private incinerators and the chemicals spewing out of dirty city chimneys, all add to the problem. But the main purveyor of harm is the automobile—"Public Health Enemy Number One."[18]

Chapter Two

Detroit's Reaction

Dr. John Middleton, director of the National Center for Air Pollution Control in the Department of Health, Education, and Welfare, wrote in 1968, "Rather than solving the vehicular pollution problem, the current and proposed standards will merely keep it from getting worse."[1] As the number of automobiles in use keeps increasing, however, the current and proposed means of control may not even do that.

In 1951, Dr. A. J. Haagen-Smit, a biochemistry professor at the California Institute of Technology, provided the first real proof that automobile emissions contribute to air pollution. It had long been thought that there was some link between automotive exhaust gases and the steadily worsening state of the air, but, until Haagen-Smit's experiments, the extent of the contribution to smog from cars was unclear.

Haagen-Smit, who now serves as chairman of the California State Air Resources Board, exposed the exhaust gases from an automobile to sunlight in his laboratory. He found that the resulting mixture irritated the eyes, damaged vegetation, corroded metals and cracked rubber—all phenomena that were attributed to smog. It even looked and smelled like the haze that was coming more and more to cover nearby Los Angeles. Together with findings by the Los Angeles Air Pollution Control District, Haagen-Smit's work led to the conclusion that automobiles contributed significantly to smog. Within a short time, it was established that car emissions were the major source of air pollution in the Los Angeles area.

The automobile manufacturers at first ignored the findings. "They said virtually that the automobile does not even produce air pollution," recalls Kenneth Hahn, then as now a member of the Los Angeles County Board of Supervisors, who began writing to Detroit in 1953, "and that the good automobile, the new one, doesn't smoke, and their research departments were not even interested in equipping a car with a device to control emissions."[2] Even after the link between autos and pollution was irrefutably established, they claimed that there was no way to limit the emissions.

California had to work on its own. Practically all the stationary sources of pollution in California had been brought under some kind of control, so technical advisory groups were set up to look for technically and economically feasible ways to control auto emissions. On the

basis of their studies, the California legislature took up
the matter. Urged on by the Los Angeles County Board
of Supervisors, the state officials began to set up procedures. It was decided that as soon as two devices could
be certified by the state pollution agency (then called
the Motor Vehicle Pollution Control Board) as capable
of reducing hydrocarbon emissions by 80 per cent and
carbon monoxide emissions by 60 per cent, all new cars
sold in California would be required to have them. The
state also required all new cars to have crankcase control
devices.

The auto companies had made the "discovery" a year
earlier, in 1959, that crankcase emissions contributed
heavily to pollution (although it is now generally held
that only about 25 per cent of the total hydrocarbons and
none of the other pollutants are emitted from the crankcase area on an uncontrolled automobile). The auto
companies announced that they would voluntarily control these so-called blowby emissions. They were doing it
on their own; the California law was, they said, "simply
coincidental."[3] (It is interesting to note that the crankcase control devices, which recirculate the escaping
gases and unburned hydrocarbons through the engine
system, had been used on older model cars to improve
engine ventilation. The auto companies were merely
putting something back on their cars that they had previously had.)

The Pollution Control Board received four devices that
could curb exhaust emissions, all submitted by companies outside the automotive industry. One was from
the American Machine and Foundry and Chromalloy
Corporation and the others were from hardware-type
companies which had teamed up with chemical firms.
They were all found to satisfy the requirements of the
legislation and were approved. But the auto companies

would have no part of them. They were not about to put some other company's control device on their cars.

As they have so often in the battle for cleaner air, the auto companies—after being pressed—backed down. Even though they had maintained that exhaust emissions could not be reduced, they finally managed to find a way to clean up, to some extent, the process of combustion inside the engine. The companies that had submitted the control devices were left out in the cold, an experience that has made it less inviting for other nonautomotive firms to take on Detroit's giants in the reduction of emissions. The precedent has also made it difficult for state and federal officials to make the auto companies do anything they do not want to do.

There are indications that the situation may be changing. The Los Angeles County Board of Supervisors in 1965 called on the U. S. Attorney General to investigate a possible conspiracy among the auto companies in their work on pollution control. The Board also asked the Attorney General to "institute an action for the purpose of preventing further conclusive obstruction to the control of air pollution from motor vehicles by the Automobile Manufacturers Association."[4]

It took a long time, but in January 1969 the conclusion of that investigation was a suit filed by the Justice Department in Los Angeles against General Motors, Ford, Chrysler, American Motors, and the AMA (Automobile Manufacturers Association). The suit charged that the auto companies had conspired with one another to suppress information on and development of control apparatus. The companies had agreed in 1953 that all work on pollution control would be industry-wide; no company would advertise its emission control work or withhold any advances from the others. The auto companies claimed that their agreement helped them reduce emis-

sions sooner than would otherwise have been possible,
but the government thought differently. The suit charged
that on several occasions the auto companies had had
technology available to reduce emissions but refused to
use it. One company, the suit said, had the control mechanisms ready for installation but did not install until the
others were also able to meet the requirements. The government ordered that the companies break up the conspiracy and cross-licensing agreements that had been in
effect. No other punishment was meted out to the auto
companies.

Detroit's officials have said that the order will slow
down their work on pollution control. That seems unlikely, but still it is questionable what will be the result
of the government's action. Perhaps it will undermine
confidence in the auto companies' ability and desire to
combat pollution. They have been telling us ever more
frequently in the face of talk about electric and steam
cars that the problem is under control. They have said
that they would be willing to meet any practicable
standard set up by federal or state officials. The Justice
Department's action might make many people wary of
these claims, for the problem is not under control. The
present methods—further and further controls on emissions from internal combustion engines—are not working
as well as had been planned; they are, as Dr. John Middleton says, just keeping the problem from getting worse.
Since the constant increase in the number of automobiles
is almost certain to offset any gains in control, only a
new way of powering a car offers a real solution.

The pollutants emitted from automobiles are the result
of incomplete combustion—that is, some of the gasoline
that is supplied to the engine is not burned or only partially burned. This unburned residue is composed of
harmful contaminants—carbon monoxide, hydrocarbon

compounds, and lesser amounts of other substances. The high combustion temperatures inside the engine cause the nitrogen and oxygen in the air to combine and form nitric oxide, another major pollutant. The rapid cooling that follows prevents the nitric oxide from decomposing and leads to further reactions, including the formation of nitrogen dioxide.

The amount of each pollutant emitted varies with the driving conditions. During acceleration and cruising—the times of heavy-load engine demand and higher combustion temperatures—the emissions of oxides of nitrogen are highest. The carbon monoxide and hydrocarbon emissions are highest during idling and deceleration, times of light-load engine demand. This means that on freeways, where there is a predominance of cruising and acceleration, the oxides of nitrogen emissions will be highest, while in stop-and-go city driving, greater amounts of carbon monoxide and hydrocarbons will be spewed out of exhausts. More total pollutants are emitted during idling and deceleration than during cruising and acceleration—something like two or three times as much. Because both the types and amounts of pollutants vary under different driving conditions, it is very difficult to design control devices that can effectively prevent all the contaminants from entering the air.

All present-day automobiles, buses, and trucks have internal combustion engines that are powered by the combustion of a mixture of gasoline or diesel oil and air inside the combustion chambers of the cylinders. Most car engines have four, six, or eight cylinders, working on the standard four-stroke cycle. On one stroke (intake), the fuel-air mixture is drawn into the cylinder above the piston; on the second stroke (compression), the mixture is compressed by the piston's upward motion and ignited; on the third (ignition), the mixture, exploding, forces the

piston downward with the power that drives the crankshaft; and on the fourth stroke (exhaust), the piston
moves upward to push the spent mixture (composed of
the unburned and partially burned pollutants) out
through the exhaust.

A variety of factors determine which pollutants will be
emitted through the exhaust. The composition of the fuel
decides which kinds of hydrocarbon compounds are
emitted. (Gasoline is made up of hydrocarbons and other
substances, like lead, that are added for increased performance.)

The amount of carbon monoxide is largely determined
by the ratio of air to fuel in the mixture supplied by the
carburetor to the cylinders. At a ratio of about 14.7
pounds of air per pound of fuel, all the gasoline would be
burned and there would be no unburned hydrocarbons or
any carbon monoxide to escape through the exhaust.
Only carbon dioxide, water, and nitrogen—all essentially
harmless—would be emitted in an ideal combustion
process.[5] But even complete combustion would result in
nitrogen oxide emissions because of the high temperatures inside the engine.

Unfortunately, the engine does not perform well at
high air-fuel ratios, so richer mixtures must be used; that
is, the air-fuel ratio is usually a good deal less than 14.7
to 1, varying anywhere from 12 to 1 in average engines to
14 or 14.5 to 1 in high-performance engines. One method
of controlling emissions is to develop engines that will
perform satisfactorily with higher air-fuel ratios. But
such methods cannot completely solve the problem.

Crankcase control devices recirculate the hydrocarbons that otherwise would escape unburned from the
car. They have been required on all new cars beginning
with the 1961 models in California and the 1964 models
nationwide. California has also required that crankcase

devices be installed on all used cars when they change hands. There is a question as to how effective these devices are. They do eliminate the pollution emanating from the crankcase by sending the hydrocarbons back through the engine system, but it is not clear how much of this unburned gasoline later escapes still unburned through the exhaust.

In 1970, California will require emission controls for evaporative losses from the fuel tank, which in hot weather can contribute as much as 15 per cent of the total hydrocarbon emissions. Some evaporative losses also occur from the carburetor.

All new cars since the 1966 models in California and 1968 models nationwide have had to meet exhaust emission standards. There will be no standard for oxides of nitrogen until 1971 models, and then only for California cars. Since emissions of nitrogen oxides increase as the temperatures of combustion increase, the higher temperatures that have accompanied most of the methods used to curb hydrocarbon and carbon monoxide emissions have actually increased pollution from oxides of nitrogen.

The auto companies themselves admit that there are limits to the present approach and that they may not be able to eliminate harmful emissions from an internal combustion engine. At hearings held in May 1968 by the Senate Commerce Committee and Air and Water Pollution Subcommittee of the Public Works Committee, Senator Howard Baker of Tennessee asked Herbert L. Misch, Ford's vice-president for engineering, about this. Baker had been told at a previous hearing that for Los Angeles to have really clean air, it would be necessary to limit hydrocarbon emissions to 35 parts per million from motor vehicles, or, at least, to something lower than the 65 parts per million that Ford has established as its lowest limit. The standards for 1968 vary with the size of the engine, but the lowest standard for hydrocarbons is 275 ppm. Baker asked Misch whether he could envision building an engine with "any devices or combination of devices that would reduce the level of unburned hydrocarbons to 35 parts per million." Misch replied: "I don't have any reason to believe that it would be possible to get that low." Many people in and out of the auto industry also doubt whether satisfactory levels for carbon monoxide and oxides of nitrogen will be attainable. One federal official has indicated that, by 1980, if the standards for 1970 cars are still in effect and the number of cars increases as is expected, the quality of the air will actually be worse than it is today. "Obviously," he says, "we have to look at alternative sources of power."[6]

Besides the doubt that internal combustion engines' emissions can ever be reduced to a satisfactory level, there are a variety of other factors, such as high cost for control devices, maintenance, inspection difficulties, effects of emission controls on engine performance, durability, and complexity of controls, that present very important problems. Why, then, have pollution authorities sought to improve the air by controlling the emissions from internal combustion engines?

For one thing, such methods are undoubtedly the easiest and require the least change throughout the society. Emission controls have been the most readily available means to keep air pollution from getting worse. Controlling the internal combustion engine was the most obvious thing to try, but progress has been slight and unpromising.

There is the problem of technological feasibility. A control device that would completely eliminate hydrocarbons would be unlikely, to say the least, to reduce oxides of nitrogen. Rather, such a device would be likely to increase emissions of nitrogen oxides. As S. Smith Griswold, formerly of the Los Angeles Air Pollution Control District and later chief of the abatement branch of the National Center for Air Pollution Control, said in December 1966 at the National Conference on Air Pollution:

> As the hydrocarbon and carbon monoxide base line emissions have gone down, the nitric oxide base line has gone up. Emission control criteria limiting the content of toxic components in the controlled exhaust have proven to be ineffective in preventing an increase in nitric oxide emissions to the atmosphere.[7]

Griswold was merely calling for a national standard for oxides of nitrogen, and the auto companies were ready. One of their spokesmen, Charles Heinen, Chrysler's chief of Emission Control, has said that "it looks like the increase in oxides of nitrogen might turn out to be a damn good thing, particularly when coupled with the reduction in hydrocarbons."[8]

The actual effects of nitrogen oxides are difficult to assess because of the nature of the chemical reaction involved. Heinen and others claim that a slight decrease in nitrogen oxides emissions will result in an increase in the ozone levels, while a slight increase in nitrogen oxides emissions may have the effect of lowering the levels of ozone. The evidence, however, seems to indicate that oxides of nitrogen are not really a "damn good thing." Pollution authorities of practically every variety outside Detroit feel that increasing oxides of nitrogen emissions can be very dangerous indeed. It may be suspected that the auto companies are against a standard because they will be hard put to meet it—as Heinen said in late 1967, the "technical status is grim." There is a "serious question as to whether you're going to get what you want."[9]

While the nitrogen oxides cannot make ozone without hydrocarbons to react with, there is still no reason to think that the nitrogen oxides are not harmful in their own right. One nitrogen oxide, nitrogen dioxide, can be lethal at high enough concentrations. At lesser levels, oxides of nitrogen are known to destroy plants and reduce resistance to respiratory illnesses.[10]

Far from believing that nitrogen oxides are harmless, Griswold holds that they can do no good at all. Those arguing against a standard to limit the pollutant, he says, claim that "its implementation will result in an increase in ozone in those areas where oxides of nitrogen are high. Well, in Los Angeles, where nitric oxide emissions have risen relative to hydrocarbon emissions during the past six years, there has been no abatement in the frequency or intensity of ozone attacks."[11]

As yet, no device to control nitrogen oxide emissions has met the standards of the California Air Resources Board. It seems likely that any such device that can be used in addition to hydrocarbon and carbon monoxide control devices will be very costly and unwieldy. As emission requirements get lower and lower, the control mechanisms get more complex, costlier, more difficult to maintain, and much harder to keep operating at top level. As Middleton says, "It is probable . . . that ultimately a limit will be reached beyond which further reductions [in internal combustion engine emissions] are technically or economically out of the question."[12]

Perhaps more important than their high cost and technical limitations is the poor operating record to date of emission control devices. They have proved difficult to maintain and not very effective in bettering the quality of the air in the areas where they have been in use for several years. By law in California, the devices are required to stay in perfect shape for 12,000 miles, but the evidence seems to indicate that the devices' effectiveness has steadily worsened after that number of miles. The California experience also suggests that the devices deteriorate with time, even if the mileage is not high. According to Miles L. Brubacher of the Air Resources Board, "Time has an important effect on vehicle emissions as well as mileage. In other words, it appears that vehicles with low rates of mileage accumulation have higher emissions."[13]

The short trip to the grocery store and other kinds of stop-and-go driving has a worsening effect on emissions. A car that has "only been driven by a little old lady to church on Sunday" is often the worst kind of polluter since it is likely to have a greater amount of harmful deposits on all components of the engine system. Brubacher says, "Carburetor and combustion chamber deposits are known to raise emissions."[14] Furthermore, stop-and-go driving can also build up deposits on emission control devices themselves, and decrease their effectiveness.

Maintenance is another serious problem affecting the efficiency of emission control apparatus. "Most mechanics," says John Maga, executive officer of the Air Resources Board (which, in 1967, replaced the Motor Vehicle Pollution Control Board), "only know how to improve an engine's performance, and usually the adjustments they make do not help emissions. In fact, emissions are sometimes increased by improper maintenance." Brubacher, the Board's chief engineer, agrees. "The data indicate," he wrote in 1968, "that service personnel are further maladjusting the cars." In a paper that he and J. C. Raymond, also of the Air Resources Board staff, presented at that year's meeting of the Air Pollution Control Association (believe it or not, the 1968 meeting was that body's 61st annual conference on air pollution control), Brubacher said that improper adjustments of "spark timing, idle speed, and idle air-fuel ratio have substantial effects on emissions."[15] As with inspection, however, the costs of training mechanics to deal with a car's emissions are quite high, says Maga, and of questionable value.

Indeed, the lack of inspection for emission controls is another drawback with the current methods. In California, there is no form of inspection for emissions whatever, although the state Highway Patrol does make spot checks to make sure that the car owners keep the control apparatus on their cars. Although most Californians do keep the devices on, the slight decrease in pollution levels strongly indicates that the devices are not working as they should. Past procedures also have permitted large numbers of cars to enter California that were unable to meet the emission standards.

The California technique is to check a small number of prototype cars each year for emissions on the auto companies' proving grounds. The state makes sure that the prototype cars meet the emissions levels for each pollutant. Tests are made by the auto companies and then the cars are re-checked by the federal government's laboratory in Ypsilanti, Michigan. Some prototypes are also driven 50,000 miles very quickly and are then tested for emissions to ensure that the emission performance of the cars and the devices does not deteriorate.

This method has its problems. First of all, the cars tested are not production-line vehicles; they are, as Maga says, "practically handmade." Therefore they perform much better than the average car that will come off an assembly line. Also, the 50,000 miles of the endurance tests, which are supposed to determine whether cars will meet emission standards after they have accumulated considerable mileage, are built up "in a hurry," Maga says, "which can't at all duplicate normal driving conditions."[16] Maga points out that a "car can deteriorate in any number of ways through private driving, and the [testing of] prototype cars can't begin to correspond with those conditions." He says that the emissions should be measured from cars off the production line, because "all cars that are sold to the public come off the production line." But, testing assembly-line cars for emissions is impractical, "since you can't tell the auto companies that their cars aren't approved after they've already gone through a production run." Is it possible to find a fair way to test cars for emissions? Maga says that the Air Resources Board is trying to find the most equitable way, both for the auto companies and for the quality of the air. "It's not a simple, straightforward thing," he says, "to determine which cars meet the emission standards."

But even if the cars can be adequately tested before coming into California, any system of periodic inspection presents great problems. One difficulty in devising such a system has to do with the "averaging" concept that has been used in California. Under this arrangement, some cars will be over the standard, others will be under. Taking averaging into account, then, there seems to be no way to inspect auto emissions that would not penalize the luckless car owner who happened to buy a car that was a bit over the emission standards.

But even if all cars were required to meet a certain standard and testing procedures could be devised to check production line cars for emissions, inspection still would be difficult to implement. Some states, particularly New Jersey which has a federal grant to experiment with emissions inspection, have periodic safety inspection programs, to which it is possible—but still costly—to add a three- or four-minute emission test. But many other states, including California, do not have safety inspections, and the financial costs of initiating an independent emission inspection program in those states would be intimidating. States that have never instituted safety inspection programs then must suffer in the battle for clean air.

California pollution authorities have considered inspection problems through the years but have not come close to a solution. Maga says that they have thought about three possible types of inspection. The simplest would be an expanded visual inspection, the sort of thing the Highway Patrol now does on a random basis. The benefits of this approach are questionable.

A second proposal is that cars should be required to have an annual adjustment of their smog control systems. But, as Maga says, this would be very expensive. Training would be needed for the mechanics, and licensing arrangements would have to be made with service stations. It would, says Maga, "take a major program."

A third approach would be built around a "black box" —a machine that could test a car's emission levels in a matter of minutes. Such a device is currently being tested in New Jersey. It is expected to be able to test smoke, carbon monoxide, and hydrocarbons in ninety seconds.[17] But mechanics still would have to be trained to adjust engines and their devices for emission control, assuming that adjustments could be devised that could bring emissions down to a certain level. Maga concludes that "the costs don't seem to be worth the benefits for air pollution."

Despite the many difficulties, an inspection system could be set up in every state. But, once again, the costs would be very great. If an automobile could be made that would produce practically no pollutants without controls, then an inspection would become unnecessary. All the other problems of the current methods of control— technical, economic, practical problems—would be solved as well.

The success of the emission control programs to date

has been insignificant. "In the long run, I'm optimistic," says Maga, who has been trying to solve the problem almost since it began, "but it means you have to tell the people in Los Angeles to suffer with smog for another ten years, maybe more. That's a long time."

In 1967, Maga says, the Los Angeles area had a 6 per cent reduction in hydrocarbon levels. Maga and the chairman of the Air Resources Board, Dr. Haagen-Smit, who started it all almost twenty years ago, feel that the present control methods will eventually be able to solve the problem, but their enthusiasm is tempered. "There will be temporary relief in the middle 70's to 80's," says Haagen-Smit, but he believes that the situation will then deteriorate again if further controls are not imposed.[18] "Under present methods," Maga says, "it is just not possible to solve this thing quickly."

Others do not share even the guarded optimism of Maga and Haagen-Smit. Dr. John Goldsmith, who has been doing research for over a decade at the California State Department of Public Health's laboratories at Berkeley, recently wrote, "Control systems installed in new cars decline in effectiveness with use. This decline, along with an increase in the number of motor vehicles, could neutralize a control system which applied only to new cars."[19]

For a variety of reasons—some touched on in this chapter—it seems doubtful whether any goal aimed at further taming the internal combustion engine, will be attained. But even if the technical goals were reached, we can see that the ultimate goal—clean air—will be even harder to attain, fraught as it is with all sorts of other problems. Some pollution authorities—men who have devoted a good part of their lives to developing control systems and trying to make them work better—feel that the current methods will be enough. They feel

that the poisons will be eliminated from our air if we
continue to develop the methods that have been used in
the past.

That, however, would seem to be taking a tremendous
risk, considering the many and expensive problems still
to be overcome. A more productive way to proceed, it
would seem, would be to look for alternative means of
powering a road vehicle, ways that do not emit any pollutants into the air but are competitive with internal
combustion engines.

Right now the technology exists that can practically
eliminate the problem of automotive pollution. Smogfree
cars, driven by modern and highly advanced steam engines, are presently being developed and tested. Indeed,
they could be on the market very soon, able to compete
in performance with anything powered by an internal
combustion engine.

Steam-powered automobiles are the nearest thing to an
immediate solution to the air pollution problem that has
yet been proposed; but the auto companies are critical.
They talk of the potential for steam cars as if it were still
the 1910's. Ford's vice-president, Mr. Misch, said at the
1968 Senate hearings on steam, "It would take considerably more leadtime to design, develop, and test a completely new powerplant and get it into production in
quantities that would be meaningful than to pursue the
improvements in the internal combustion engine." Or as
Henry Ford II has put it, somewhat less diplomatically,
"We have tremendous investment in facilities for engines,
transmissions, and axles, and I can't see throwing these
away just because the electric car doesn't emit fumes."[20]

Faced by increasingly strong pressure to clean up his
cars' pollution, however, Ford publicly has modified his
stand. In December 1969 his company committed $60
million to a two-year program to find ways of reducing

automotive pollution and Ford was quoted by the Associated Press as saying, "We have a strong vested interest in the survival of the internal combustion engine, but we have a far stronger interest in the survival of our company. It would be foolhardy for us to stand by and let others take the lead in efforts to make the internal combustion engine obsolete." Whether such a statement represents any real change in company policy, however, remains to be seen.

The auto companies do some work with steam, and General Motors has entered into agreements with steam engineers to have cars made for them. But GM's vice-president for research, Lawrence Hafstad, said at the Senate hearings, "The operating problems and problems of cost and the bulk of the steam engine will be so high that probably the gas engine will come out ahead." And the agreement has been made with Besler Development, Oakland, California, which supplied GM with information used at the Senate hearings. Hafstad said George Besler of that firm felt that cost, boiler size, and maintenance were significant problems that steam had to overcome. Such statements do not indicate an optimistic attitude on the subject. When GM exhibited two steam cars in mid-1969—one designed by Besler—the company stressed the problems more than the advantages.

Ford's "research" procedures have taken a different shape, but their point of view seems no more constructive than GM's. Ford has given a $2.2 million contract to Thermo Electron Corporation, Waltham, Massachusetts, to develop steam engines—but not for automotive use. Before the contract was made with Ford, Thermo Electron's steam people were seriously thinking about automotive applications for the steam system they were working on. They supplied a paper, "Advanced Steam Engines for Automotive Use," to the Morse panel on electrically-powered vehicles, and saw no problems in converting the small engine they were developing to larger sizes. Since that time, Theodore Johnson, Thermo Electron's vice-president, has become convinced that steam cars "will only be produced by the big auto companies." (Nevertheless in June 1969 Thermo Electron was awarded a contract by the National Center for Air Pollution Control to make designs of a steam-powered passenger car. Eventually, the company might produce a prototype steam car —probably no sooner than 1975.)

Fortunately, steam engine development is not going to be left to the auto companies. Too many people—prominent people with money and government officials, at both the state and federal levels—are interested in steam to let the "auto companies bury steam the way they've done before," as one steam-engine developer has put it.[21] This time steam will not be prejudged; it will be given a chance to show whether or not it can solve the air pollution problem.

The low pollution characteristics of steam-powered vehicles are well known, even to the auto companies. Because it burns all of its fuel in a complete combustion process and because its fuel requires no additives, a steam car emits much less pollution into the air. And the low pollution characteristics of a steam car do not deteriorate as they do on internal combustion engine vehicles. At the Senate hearings, GM's Hafstad was asked by Senator James Pearson of Kansas, "We are told that the existing pollution control devices on the internal combustion engines lose their effectiveness over a period of time. Do the steam engines have a comparable problem?"

Mr. Hafstad replied: "No, because built into the combustion system of any one of these three low emission engines you have continuous combustion, they run continuously, no variation up and down the way an automobile does, and for that reason they can be essentially adjusted for optimum combustion conditions."

A steam car built at Ambler, Pennsylvania, by the Williams Engine Company (which has since gone out of business) was tested in January 1967 for emissions at the Mobil Oil Testing Laboratory in Paulsboro, New Jersey. The car, then seven years old and with about 25,000 miles on it, had no control devices and no attempt was made to make the emissions any lower than they would be during normal driving. It was found to emit 20 parts per million hydrocarbons, one-twentieth of one per cent carbon monoxide, and 40 ppm oxides of nitrogen. By comparison, the lowest goals that Ford engineers are attempting, according to Mr. Misch at the Senate hearings, are 65 ppm hydrocarbons, three-tenths (six-twentieths) of one per cent carbon monoxide, and 175 ppm oxides of nitrogen—goals that have not yet been reached, even in the laboratory. As mentioned earlier, the way to meet those goals is not yet in sight. For uncontrolled internal combustion engine automobiles of medium size, incidentally, the emissions are about 1,000 ppm hydrocarbons and 1,500 ppm oxides of nitrogen.

All the problems of emission control that still must be solved will be eliminated by steam cars. The maintenance, loss of performance, durability, cost, inspection, testing, and technical problems could be forgotten. As Calvin Williams of the Williams Engine Company said at the Senate hearings:

> Low emission is not an option with steam power. It is built in, requiring no "clean air packages," expensive catalytic mufflers, or other devices whose complexity requires tuning and maintenance. Nobody can remove steam's inherent superiority with a 39 cent screwdriver—as is often done by a disgruntled cus-

tomer or dealer, who doesn't like the driveability price which must be paid when these devices are installed and used correctly.

It has been difficult to control the emissions from internal combustion engines. There are many problems that must be solved before the air will benefit significantly from the current methods of control. Emission levels from internal combustion engines are high and can be lowered somewhat with control devices. But improvement in air quality is still a long way in the future at the present rate of progress. To quote Calvin Williams again: "We don't hope to reach these figures sometime in the 1970's; we know that we can begin to reduce Los Angeles' motor vehicle smog level not to 1940, but to almost zero—tomorrow—given the opportunity."

Chapter Three

The Steam Car Historically

Not many years ago, the idea of using any form of power other than steam to move a road vehicle was inconceivable. Indeed, it may be argued that steam-powered vehicles did not fade out because of any demonstrated inferiority to cars driven by internal combustion engines, but rather because of a complex set of historical and psychological factors that worked to the benefit of gas vehicles and against the fortunes of steam cars. While examining these factors, it is important to place the American automotive revolution in historical perspective.

Steam was first used to power a road vehicle in 1769 when Nicholas Joseph Cugnot, French army engineer, designed a three-wheeled truck to haul heavy artillery. It was a bulky, unwieldy machine, with the boiler, firebox, and machinery all attached above and to the front of the single front wheel. To turn the truck, it was necessary to pivot the entire engine system, which made maneuvering difficult. Two of these contraptions were built (one is now on display in Paris)—both on an experimental basis at the expense of the French war ministry.

Some historians have tended to glamorize Cugnot's machine, and facts are hard to come by. It seems that the truck could travel at speeds of three miles an hour and carry loads of three-and-a-half tons. Unlike most of the other steam engines of that era—such as the early ones developed by Thomas Newcomen and James Watt which used the steam only to create a vacuum by condensation —Cugnot's was a two-cylinder engine run by high-pressure steam formed expansively without condensation.

Like many of its successors, Cugnot's machine needed almost constant refueling, and its heavy boiler and firebox made it very hard to handle. On its second test run, the vehicle ran into a wall and turned over. The war ministry then decided to give up the project.

Throughout the nineteenth century, the development of road vehicles took second place to the burgeoning railroad industry. In England, this second-place position of automobiles, or carriages as they were called, was reflected in discriminatory tolls and legislation. But some inventors still managed to devise interesting machines. Richard Trevithick, whose work encompassed practically every aspect of steam power in the first quarter of the nineteenth century, was one of the first and most famous builders of steam carriages. In 1801, Trevithick's first vehicle climbed a steep hill with a full load on Christmas Eve before being driven back to its shed, where both the vehicle and building caught fire and were destroyed.

He built another carriage two years later and a third in 1808. The latter may have been driven to London from Cornwall, although one historian[1] cites the bad roads in England at that time and the vehicle's need for water and fuel every few miles as reasons for supposing that the vehicle was "probably sent by sea." Trevithick's carriages were run by noncondensing high pressure boilers, similar to Cugnot's. But, also like Cugnot's, Trevithick's carriages ran into problems. In London, Trevithick drove through a fence and interest died in his venture. Lacking money to pursue his work on carriages, Trevithick set to work on railway locomotives, but again an accident kept the innovative inventor from seeing his project come into general use.

It was another ten or fifteen years before carriages began to appear in any numbers in the English countryside. For a time only experimental models were built. But by the late 1820's and 1830's, a large number of steam carriages were making regular passenger runs between towns, like buses.

These machines had very high-pressure boilers, whose pressures sometimes reached as high as 200 pounds per square inch, compared with the 50 pounds or so that was normal in the early locomotive boilers. Perhaps the most advanced of these coaches was one built in the mid-1830's by W. H. James. It had a four-cylinder engine, with the cylinders paired off—each pair independently working one driving wheel, which made it much easier to turn corners. James's vehicle also had a three-speed variable gear system and a properly sprung rear axle for a much more comfortable ride than on the other coaches of the day.

As more steam coaches were built and put into public use, they were increasingly opposed by railway and stagecoach associations. In 1831 a special committee was established by the Parliament to look into the dangers and benefits of the steam vehicles. The committee—after hearing evidence from all sides—reported favorably on the steam carriages. It recommended the abolition of high tolls on the vehicles, and urged the Parliament to enact various measures to encourage their development. But pressure from various groups—primarily the railroad and stagecoach interests—forced Parliament to follow a different course, and that body soon passed restrictive tolls and legislation aimed at suppressing the road vehicles.

Some of the opposition stemmed from traditional English conservatism. "Steam-carriages were strongly opposed by country gentlemen," writes one chronicler, "and it is said that no fewer than forty bills were presented to the Parliament for the purpose of having them removed from common roads."[2] The coaches were said to frighten horses—and people as well.

But there were other factors that led to steam's demise in early nineteenth century England:

> King William's government was preoccupied with the struggle over the Reform Bill, politicians and public alike were convinced that a revolution was at hand, and such capitalists as were ready to invest in new industries were more easily tempted by the railways than by the road steamers.[3]

The Parliamentary commission reported that the carriages were technically advanced and safe and that they were not nuisances to the public. If they had continued to be developed, the steam carriages might have marked the beginning of an automotive industry some sixty years before such an industry actually got under way. But in

1840 a boiler exploded on one of the coaches, killing five passengers and injuring twenty others. This accident had considerable public impact, and, together with the other factors mentioned above, led Parliament to attempt to legislate the steamers off the road.

Most of the prohibitory legislation was in the form of tolls: a driver of a steam vehicle had to pay a good deal more to traverse a road than did a horse-drawn coach driver. Steamers were also required to be accompanied by an attendant, who would walk ahead of the carriage carrying a red flag. The coaches, which could average about ten miles an hour, soon began to fade from the roads.

In America, the situation was somewhat different. Although the early carriages were not so advanced as their English counterparts, the attitude of the public was a bit more favorable. Nevertheless, the available capital went into other pursuits, primarily the railroads. America did not seem to be ready for cars. Hiram Percy Maxim, one of the early experimenters with the gasoline engine, explained his view of the situation in a book published in 1937:

> It has always been my belief that we all began to work on a gasoline-propelled road vehicle at about the same time because it had become apparent that civilization was ready for a mechanical vehicle. It was natural that this idea should strike many of us at about the same time. It has been the habit to give the gasoline-engine all the credit for bringing the automobile, as we term the mechanical road vehicle today. In my opinion this is a wrong explanation. We have had the steam engine for over a century. We could have built steam vehicles in 1880, or indeed in 1870. But we did not. We waited until 1895.

According to Maxim, the reason cars were not built in large numbers before the 1890's—although various steam-powered vehicles were constructed in the previous dec-

ades—was that the bicycle "had not yet come in numbers
and had not directed men's minds to the possibilities of
independent, long-distance travel over the ordinary
highway." He went on:

> We thought the railroad was good enough. The bicycle created
> a new demand which it was beyond the ability of the railroad
> to supply. Then it came about that the bicycle could not satisfy
> the demand which it had created. A mechanically-propelled
> vehicle was wanted instead of a foot-propelled one, and we
> now know that the automobile was the answer.[4]

As interest in the automobile continued to grow, most
inventors turned their attention to a new kind of engine
that had been developed by two Germans named Otto
and Langen in 1866, an engine powered by gasoline.

At this time, the work being done by Americans was
overshadowed by the significant advances in steam car
technology that were being made in France by Leon
Serpollet. He was one of the few early steam car makers
to develop and use an *automotive* steam technology instead of borrowing the technology from steam locomotives. Serpollet developed a flash-type generator, or
boiler, in which the steam was produced as it was
needed. This eliminated the possibility of explosions
while allowing very high pressures. He also replaced the
coke-burning engines that had followed the wood-burn-
ing ones with a new engine that used oil, or paraffin, as
its fuel. His metering systems were advanced, and his
cars could outdrive anything on the road in the 1890's.

Serpollet was a poor man, however, and he was left to
fend for himself when Armand Peugeot, who had earlier
been interested in Serpollet's steam vehicles, turned to
the new Daimler gas engine. Although he had driven one
of his cars to a land speed record of 75.06 miles per hour
in 1902, Serpollet continually faced stiff competition.
When he died in 1907, his innovations seemed to die with

him as France and England turned to gasoline-powered automobiles.

Why then did steam cars fade away? It is an interesting history to trace. First there was Cugnot whose experiments were thwarted by a conservative war ministry. Then came Trevithick who ran into accidents and a lack of financial support because of them. The later English carriage-makers were countered by a growing railroad industry and political and economic factors peculiar to nineteenth-century England. At the time when the desire for automobiles was generated in this country, when the railroads made travel thinkable and the bicycle made private vehicles desirable, the only truly innovative mind was in France and belonged to a poor businessman. Here we had F. E. and F. O. Stanley, in whose hands the automotive industry in this country was probably formulated.

It is unfair to blame the Stanley twins for the demise of steam cars. After all, they did produce vehicles, which is more than can be said for a good many others, and they kept producing steamers even after other steam car makers bowed to the pressure and switched to gas. They were, perhaps, the square peg in the round hole, the wrong men for the job. When steam needed an aggressive entrepreneur who would compete on equal terms with the blossoming automotive giants, the Stanley brothers were not the right men for the task. Their story —and the stories of the other American steam car producers in the early part of this century—adds weight to the argument that steam cars were not technically inferior to gas-powered vehicles, but were simply a victim of historical accident.

In October 1896, legend tells us, F. E. (Francis) Stanley went to a fair in Brockton, Massachusetts. He was disappointed to see sickly performances there by both steam and gas cars. On the train ride back from the fair,

Stanley was asked whether he was planning to buy "one of those things." "No," he said, "I'm going to build a better one."

At first it was just a hobby. The Stanley brothers had a prosperous dry-plate photography business, and did not intend to manufacture steam cars. But they were proud men, and when they were asked to participate in a speed and hillclimbing competition in Cambridge in 1898, they couldn't refuse. Their steamer was pitted against three American cars and a De Dion racer from France.

The American cars went around the track first, followed by the French racer, which negotiated the course in record time. Then F. E. Stanley got the steam up, took off, and whizzed around the track to set a new world record. In the hillclimbing contest, the Stanleys also led the field. "In less than two weeks," F. E. said later, "we had received orders for over two hundred cars similar to the one shown there. It was then, for the first time, we decided to engage in the manufacture of automobiles."[5]

It is unlikely that the Stanley twins had ever heard of Leon Serpollet. Their cars—although radically different from the American steamers of the day—borrowed heavily from steam locomotive technology. The Stanleys managed to build an excellent automobile for its time, but it would be another fifteen years before Serpollet's principles were used in this country. By that time, the pattern had been set. By 1915, gas-driven cars had already won their place in the American heart.

The Stanley Steamer used a very simple generator— a firetube, locomotive-type boiler arranged vertically— which was light (about 90 pounds), as was the engine (which had two cylinders and weighed about 60 pounds). The boiler could hold a great deal of steam pressure—as much as 1,300 pounds per square inch— without exploding. The twins took great pleasure in demonstrating their car's safety, but the thought that steam cars were dangerous, that their boilers *could* blow up, always haunted the steamer.

There were other reasons for the death of the Stanley Steamer. For one, the twins refused to mass-produce their automobiles or to use labor-saving practices. The story has been told about a visit Henry Ford made to the Stanley plant in 1905. Ford asked the brothers how many cars they produced in a year. The Stanleys said 650, to which Ford replied, "Why, we make that many in one day in my factory."

The Stanleys were "cussed" New Englanders. They wanted to make a comfortable living and had no interest in building an automotive empire. They didn't believe in advertising: they liked to say that "our cars advertise themselves." They were individualists, not the kind of people to fight the new gas carmakers that were developing in Detroit. "A customer simply couldn't walk in and buy a Stanley Steamer," we are told, "He had to be screened, like a candidate for an exclusive club. If the Stanleys decided he didn't have the right personality for their car, they wouldn't even take his order."[6]

F. E. and F. O. were eccentric, as one writer has put it, in the traditional American sort of way. They insisted on cash payment for their cars—no credit or installment buying. They refused to restyle the car, keeping the appearance very similar year after year. It was always long, black, and frightening to behold.

They used to like to scare horses with their machine, and scare people as well. They also enjoyed the speed that their car provided, and sometimes would play on the similarity of their looks (rumor has it that they were identical twins down to the last whisker on their faces) to pull practical jokes. Once F. O. was stopped by a policeman for going too fast. No sooner had the officer begun to write out a ticket—or do whatever it was they did in those days—than F. E. whizzed by in an identical steamer, looking exactly like his brother. The policeman became so bewildered that he let both Stanleys off, just to get them out of his hair.

The Stanley Steamer was the fastest vehicle on the road for several years. In 1906, a Stanley Rocket driven by Fred Marriott, one of the twins' mechanics, set five world speed records in Daytona Beach, Florida, at one point clocking the amazing time of 127.66 miles per hour. That made Marriott the first man to go faster than two miles a minute with any machine. A year later, Marriott was seriously hurt when his car crashed on the beach at 197 m.p.h. F.E. later said, "the most valuable lesson learned was the great danger such terrific speed incurs. So we decided never again to risk the life of a courageous man for such a small return."[7]

Stories continued to spread about the Stanley Steamer. It became a legend in its own time and gave the Stanleys all the business they needed to live comfortably. Until F. E. died in 1917—at which time F. O. (Freelan) Stanley sold the company—the Stanleys produced 600 or 700 cars a year, enough to keep the Stanleys' master mechanics working steadily. The Stanley Steamer died, most probably, because of the personalities of its inventors. The twins were most assuredly not modern-minded businessmen. They even refused to equip the car with a condenser to eliminate the steam billowing from the boiler until the city governments of Boston and Chicago threatened to ban the steamer from their streets. Lacking a condensing system, the Stanley had to be refilled with water fairly often, which was yet another strike against it.

The White Steamer was produced by business-conscious men who advertised. It also performed well in competition—an ad in a 1907 *Scientific American* proudly proclaimed that the White Steamer had won a "larger percentage of victories in competition than any other five makes combined." Although other steamers were built, such as the Lane Steamer which won the 1902 New York–Buffalo endurance race, only the White was produced for a significant period of time and in large quantities.

The car was designed primarily by Rollin White, one of three sons of Thomas White, the founder of the White Sewing Machine Company. Rollin, who had had some engineering background, had been put in charge of maintaining the family car—a Stanley Steamer purchased in 1899. He began tinkering with it and soon developed a semi-flash-type generator, or boiler, something like Serpollet's, which kept the boiler from burning out as often as the early Stanleys were wont to do. But the White boiler held considerably more water than Serpollet's and so still needed frequent refilling.

After Rollin had made other improvements in the car, the Whites decided to produce their own cars. The body design was much like that of the gas cars of the day, and the condensing system, which looked much like the radiators of the gasoline vehicles, helped eliminate some of the Stanley's problems with water and city governments.

The first White car was produced in 1901. For ten years, the Whites advertised, innovated, competed, and built as many cars as they could. But in the end they didn't stay faithful to steam. As they saw gas cars become more and more popular, as service stations turned almost exclusively to servicing gas cars, and as public troughs were eliminated in more and more towns because of a hoof and mouth disease epidemic, the Whites switched to gas. They built their first gas-powered automobile in 1910 and then decided against competing with the automotive giants at all. The Whites—businessmen, first, last, and always—specialized in trucks and buses and left the steamer business to the Stanley twins.

But even as gas cars became more nearly universal, many stuck with steam. A letter-writer to *Scientific American* in 1916 was convinced that the steamer was a far better machine:

> A very good case can be made for the steamer—not only on the grounds that the steamer uses cheaper fuel, can be throttled to as low a speed as you please without loss of tractive effort, is smooth in action, and has no gear shift, though these are all points of advantage that would be proclaimed from the house tops by "gas car" drivers if they had them on their cars—but on the grounds that the steamer is a more consistent and steadier performer, its engine much more powerful and responsive to the driver's will and the car incomparably more active on the road.[8]

The early steam cars had disadvantages to be sure— slow start-up time, short water mileage, unreliable controls, problems with freezing, short-life boilers, and a reputation for needing extensive engineering knowledge to operate them. Some of these problems were over-emphasized (such as the engineering knowledge needed), and most of the others were generally dealt with by 1920 or so by inventors such as Abner Doble, E. C. Newcomb, and L. L. Scott, whose cars were all described in glowing terms in the pages of *Scientific American*. But the automobile companies were already becoming powerful. An interesting case in point is their response to the gasoline shortage during World War I. Instead of turning to steam or even considering it (already, we are to assume, the auto companies had a large investment in internal combustion engines that they were not willing to throw away because the steamer could burn cheaper fuel), the automotive manufacturers designed their cars to use a different grade of gas, which brought about discomforting complications. A low-priced, mass-produced steam car at that time might have turned the tide. But the money was not available, and the steam car-makers, notably Doble, spent their time on custom-made, highly expensive steamers that performed beautifully and flawlessly. But the average citizen could not afford a Doble. He had to buy a gas-powered car.

"I think that the comparatively small use of steam automobiles can be explained," one steam advocate wrote at the time, "by the fact that the motoring public of the present day is almost wholly ignorant concerning them." He blamed the lack of public knowledge "in large measure" on the "steam car manufacturers themselves who have been content to sell their product to the few who really appreciated them without attempting to induce others to buy."[9]

Another steam advocate said that in the long run the most advantageous route for automotive engineering to follow would be to eliminate the disadvantages of steamers rather than to add troublesome devices to the gas car. In 1919 he wrote, "With the fuel situation in its present shape, and with the desire on the part of the automobile-buying public for an automobile that will perform as only the steam cars will, it appears to be high time for the automotive engineer to be giving attention to the steam automobile."[10]

A year before, a mechanical engineer named E. T. Adams, in a paper presented at the annual meeting of the American Society of Mechanical Engineers, reflected a

similar view. He declared that steam had never been
given a real chance. Adams called the demise of steam
vehicles an accident of history. He wrote:

> In the general power field, this is the era of steam. In the
> field of automotive power, even more absolutely, this is the
> era of gasoline. The supremacy of steam for general power
> purposes has been attained only after years of competitive de-
> velopment. The gasoline engine has developed without serious
> competition and in a very short time. We therefore lack the
> assurance that its present pre-eminence in all departments of
> the automotive field may not be based on causes other than
> superior fitness for the service, such, for example, as a condi-
> tion of the oil industry, now outworn, or upon the initial un-
> readiness of other types of engines.[11]

Adams described the advantages of steam cars over
gasoline cars—simplicity of the engine (including its
lack of transmission), its high torque at low speeds
(meaning faster acceleration and greater power, which
comes in handy when climbing hills), the overload
capacity of the engine, and the smooth flexible speed and
power control. He pointed as well to the steamer's faults,
which gas car makers had been doing since the turn of
the century (and, incidentally, continue to do today).
But most, if not all, of the disadvantages had been handled by Abner Doble in the late 1910's and by Frank
Curran, who tested a steam-powered bus in 1928.

Abner Doble made a total of forty-two steamers between 1913 and 1930, when he went bankrupt and left
the country. He was, we are told, "convinced of the inherent advantages of power and flexibility of steam . . .
and was determined to apply to a steam car certain ele-
ments of quick starting . . . and ease and certainty of
control, which have made the gas car so popular."[12] According to the same magazine article written in 1916,
Doble had begun design work in 1911 and built his first

car in 1913. He first received notoriety, however, when he displayed his steamer at the 1917 New York Auto Show.

Doble retained and modified many features of the gas cars to make his automobile more workable. He kept the radiator and used the large condensing surface both for condensation and also to improve water mileage. The Doble could go over 1,000 miles (some observers have said 1,500 miles) on one twenty-five-gallon filling of water. He used a spark plug for ignition, which allowed him to bring the starting time down to less than a minute (about forty-five seconds). This could be shortened to about ten seconds if the car had been run in the past day. Doble used a lubricating oil to keep the boiler clean. The controls were reliable, and the boiler and engine were as small and longlasting as the engine system on gas cars. Freezing was not a real problem, either, since he mixed alcohol with the water to lower the freezing point.

Doble, one writer has said, was a "misguided genius." His cars were masterpieces, not really fit for the competitive market. He was also burdened by problems beyond his control. After his car was shown in 1917, he was swamped with over $27 million worth of orders, but the War Emergency Board discouraged production, and he was unable to fill any of them.

But Doble's main fault was that he was a "fit competitor for a Henry Royce," when steam needed a Henry Ford. His cars were superb pieces of machinery, everything on them practically handmade. He gave 100,000-mile guarantees on the generating system and three-year warranties on the rest of the car. Several Dobles are still running today, one reportedly with 800,000 miles on it. His cars were built to last, but the price was $11,200, not really in keeping with Henry Ford's dictum of a car in every household.

Without a Henry Ford, the steam car business faded into oblivion. During the Depression, Doble went to England to make steam trucks and was moderately successful. Also in England, Alex Moulton worked on steam cars for awhile, before he began using his engineering talents for the British Motor Company. And Frank Curran's steam bus of 1928 turned out to be another one-shot experimental steam automotive project.

In the early 1950's, steam produced a flurry of interest when Robert Paxton McCulloch established the Paxton Division of his McCulloch Motors Company. A highly successful builder of chain saws and two-cycle engines, McCulloch wanted to build the "Paxton," a high-class steam car that would make the Doble look cheap. He hired Doble as a consultant and set to work designing a car. But, after a couple of years of tinkering, McCulloch saw that it would be too expensive to compete with the giants of Detroit. He and Doble had developed a highly efficient compound engine that could start up in twenty seconds, but McCulloch felt that it would be economically too risky to produce steam cars, and so, in 1954, he discontinued his project.

Technically, the steamers—from Cugnot to McCulloch (or, at least to Doble)—were not inferior to the modes of transportation of their day. In the early years—especially after the self-starter was developed for gas cars—the slow start-up time of the steamers hurt. But that, like most of the other technical problems, had been dealt with by the 1920's. What really did in the steamers were personal idiosyncrasy, economic "facts of life," historical and psychological circumstances—the latter caused, to some degree, by unfortunate accidents with steamers, and also, indirectly, by the steamer's speed and power. Who would have been afraid of the Stanley Steamer had it not been faster than anything on the road and involved in a serious accident, an accident that even the most gas-partial observer would admit was caused by the condition of the beach and not, to any extent, by the car itself?

There is one advantage steam has over internal combustion engines that will eventually make the difference —its low pollution. Steam has never been an inferior power source. It seems to have been afflicted with an historical curse—not enough money at the proper time, freak accidents at crucial moments, no mass-production —plus aggressive competition of the automobile manufacturers who have never ceased to proclaim that the gas-driven car is the only kind to have. Almost since the turn of the century, steam cars have been thought of as something odd, something not right. That, it would seem, is something the public should have another chance to decide for itself.

A 1928 magazine description of Frank Curran's steam bus contained a prophetic observation. Writing primarily about the Curran steam engine's advantages in addition to its elimination of all the disadvantages previously attached to steam vehicles, a reporter for *Scientific American* pointed out that the Curran engine burned all its fuel *completely* (his emphasis). He closed his story with the following sentence:

> To the average person who must frequent streets which are crowded with traffic, the elimination, at least in part, of some of the obnoxious gases which are the products of combustion in the gasoline engine, will be welcomed as a wholesome boon, for clean air to breathe is rapidly becoming at a premium and no one realizes it more than he who must inhale, almost without cessation, the atmosphere which now is a part of his daily experience.[13]

The statement is no less true today than it was in 1928.

Chapter Four

The Steam Car Today

In late 1967, steam cars were rediscovered. They had been all but forgotten since McCulloch abandoned his project in 1954, and none had been made commercially since the last Doble in 1930. But as attempts at curbing emissions from automobiles proved more and more disappointing and as the condition of the air in most American cities grew progressively worse, there was renewed interest in vehicles that would not pollute the air.

The story really started a year earlier, in the summer and fall of 1966, with talk about electric cars. Articles appeared in the popular press with titles like "Volts-wagen," "Watts Happening in Autos," "Welcome Back, Electrics," and "Back to Electric Cars?" There had, of course, been articles before, such as "1960 Shapes Up as Key Year for Renaissance of the Electric Vehicle."[1] But in 1966, the urgent interest in air pollution control and traffic congestion made the articles seem more believable. The articles were accompanied by announcements from Ford and General Motors of developments in electric car research. Also, in the opinion of Richard S. Morse, who later headed a government-sponsored panel to investigate the state of the art in electric automotive technology, there was at the time "some thought that the federal government ought to make electric cars."

Four bills—two in the Senate and two in the House of Representatives—were introduced calling on the government to sponsor research and development of electrically powered automobiles. Electrics were hailed by many as the answer to smog. But some government officials—notably J. Herbert Hollomon, then the Assistant Secretary of Commerce for Science and Technology—were cautious. Hollomon and others thought that the problem should be examined thoroughly before cures were proposed. "It was a problem of such magnitude," Hollomon said later, "that it seemed desirable to create in the executive branch some mechanism of bringing to the public, the Congress, and the administration the best knowledge that we had available in this country to lay the groundwork for whatever decisions we all might like to make." The bills that had been proposed in Congress, Hollomon said, tended to prejudge the issue. Nobody knew whether electrics were a possibility worth developing or a dead end. Before allocating funds, Hollomon suggested, it might be a good idea to look at the technological questions involved.[2]

Hollomon, who left the government in 1968 to become President of the University of Oklahoma, also served as chairman of the Commerce Technical Advisory Board. With members from the scientific community, from labor groups, from industry, and from the public at large, the Advisory Board had previously sponsored large-scale studies on technical issues. It had had a hand in setting up the National Patent Commission and the Environmental Science Services Administration (ESSA) in the Department of Commerce. "It has been effective," says Morse, who has been a member for several years, "because people do not think it's prejudiced."

Hollomon turned to the board and asked it to sponsor a panel on electrically-powered vehicles. Members of the board, as well as officials in the Department of Commerce, talked to representatives from other departments and agencies; when the panel was formally set up in January 1967, the sponsors included six cabinet-level departments, plus the Atomic Energy Commission and the Federal Power Commission.

The sixteen-member panel was officially selected by John T. Connor, then the Secretary of Commerce; he was aided by Hollomon, Morse (after he was chosen to be chairman), and other members of the Advisory Board. It included men from universities and from industrial firms, both automotive and nonautomotive. There were representatives from the large auto companies and other large technically-oriented corporations as well as people from smaller firms. Morse, a government and industrial consultant associated with the Sloan School of Management at Massachusetts Institute of Technology and a former Assistant Secretary of the Army, brought to the chairmanship experience in working in academia, industry, and government.

The panel was expected to examine the problems and

possibilities of using electric cars to combat air pollution, but, as explained in the panel's report, its members soon realized that a "narrow focus on the electric vehicle would produce a report of limited usefulness."[3] The study therefore was expanded, and subpanels were established to look deeply into the question of automotive air pollution and methods of control. Morse explained, "We looked at all types of vehicles, and once and for all addressed ourselves to the detailed technological and economic problems." Over 100 people participated in the panel's investigation, all working, Morse noted, without pay.

Many agencies interested in pollution control delayed action until the report was released—the first volume in October 1967 and the second, which included the subpanel reports, in December 1967. When released, it was hailed as an impartial and comprehensive study of the state of the technology. Morse says that "a lot of people in the technical community have come up to me and said, 'Now, we know what we can do.' " The report, *The Automobile and Air Pollution: A Program for Progress*, had considerable impact. "We essentially stopped the legislation on electric cars," Morse says, pointing to the panel's finding that at the present time electric cars could be developed only for use with very limited range, "and we raised the call that there is a crisis."

Most importantly, the panel looked at steam-powered automobiles and had some good words to say about them. Morse was so impressed with the possibilities for steam power that he, David Ragone, another panel member who is now a professor at Carnegie-Mellon University in Pittsburgh, and seven others founded a company, Energy Systems, Incorporated, to make steam engines. The rest of the panel seemed as impressed with steam as were Morse and Ragone. Recognizing that there had been "relatively little industrial or government support for the development of steam engines in recent years," the panel nevertheless wrote that the "reciprocating steam engine power plant may be a reasonable alternative to the internal combustion engine, in terms of meeting both performance and emission requirements."[4] The panel found difficulties with every other power source proposed to replace the gas engine. There were problems with turbines, with cutting emissions to reasonable limits on the internal combustion engine, with battery powered electric cars, with machines powered by fuel cells, and with hybrid systems. Steam, concluded the Morse panel, was a viable alternative. Although only a minimum amount of money had been expended on steam research and development in recent years in contrast to the expenditures on gas, turbine, and electric engines, steam seemed to be able to meet both emission and performance requirements of advanced automotive use. It was a powerful and influential recommendation.

Another report that appeared a little later than the Morse panel's study spoke just as favorably, if not more so, about steam for automotive use. *Technology and Urban Transportation: Environmental Quality Considerations*, which came out in January 1968 in limited supply at the Hudson Institute in New York, was the work of Robert U. Ayres, who had moved from the Hudson Institute to Resources for the Future, Incorporated, in Washington. Ayres, who now is vice-president for International Research and Technology, a small research firm in Washington, D. C., spent a year and a half examining the interaction between transportation and the environment. Ayres had originally viewed his study as an investigation of alternate forms of automotive power, "principally a study of the feasibility of electric cars," but he soon became interested in other possibilities—notably steam.

"I went to Europe in May of 1967," Ayres said; "I had gone to look at the Stirling engine at the Philipps Company in Holland." (The Stirling is an external combustion engine related to steam; most experts feel that it is too large and heavy for automotive use but some think it could eventually be developed for use in trucks and buses.) "One weekend I was on the boat going up the Rhine, where I met an American. We started talking, I told him what I was doing, and he mentioned the Steam Car Club of America. I remembered something about a Doble, but that was as much as I knew about steam cars at the time."

When Ayres returned to this country, he wrote to the Steam Automobile Club, a Chicago-based organization whose members include both connoisseurs of vintage steamers and persons interested in building, developing, or owning a modern steam car. The group publishes a magazine on a somewhat regular basis. From the club Ayres learned about the Williams brothers and other inventors and tinkerers who were doing work with steam. "I visited all the people who were working on steam systems," Ayres said, "and pretty much examined the state of the art. By the time I wrote my report, I was convinced that steam cars were the nearest thing to an immediate answer to the problem of automotive air pollution."

Ayres' belief was reflected in his report. He devoted an entire chapter to steam engine technology, concentrating on the technical aspects of the modern steam automobile, what was required and what was now available. At about the same time, *Road Test* magazine also made a thorough investigation of steam. Its December 1967 issue featured a long history of steam cars and a rundown of current activities. Compiled and written by the magazine's staff, the article said that "there is no doubt that the tech-

nology is here today to build a steam-powered car equal
to or better than the I. C. [internal combustion] engine
car. And most important, it is a rapid, practical solution
to our serious air pollution problems."⁵ On the basis of
that article, the California State Assembly's Committee
on Transportation and Commerce held hearings in
March 1968 on alternate forms of automotive power,
and, as a result of those hearings, the California legislature instituted a testing program of steam powered vehicles, which will be discussed later.

As more studies and reports were submitted, there was
increased optimism about the possibilities of steam. More
people began to hear about steam. In early 1967 the National Center for Air Pollution Control contracted two
studies, one by Arthur D. Little, Incorporated, on electric cars, and the other by the Battelle Institute on all
other forms of automotive power. The Battelle investigation was originally planned to deal with atomic and nuclear powered cars and other modes of power suitable for
the year 2001, and the report was entitled "Study of Unconventional Thermal, Mechanical, and Nuclear Low-
Pollution-Potential Power Sources for Urban Vehicles."
But, in fact, the nine Battelle investigators found nothing
"unconventional" about steam, except that it was viable
and practical. Like the Morse panel, Ayres, and the *Road
Test* research staff, the Battelle people wrote favorably
about steam. As a result, the National Center has become
interested in steam developments.

Nevertheless, difficulties remained. Most of the work
being done was in backyards by independent inventors.
Taken together, all the steam projects might possibly
have resulted in a modern car. But they were all different. As the *Road Test* article noted, "Each one is working
on his own pet project and no two are alike. Conse-

quently each one is having technical problems with one or more important parts of the total system."[6]

In hopes of discovering the true potential of steam, the Senate Commerce Committee and Air and Water Pollution Subcommittee of the Public Works Committee held hearings in May 1968 on the feasibility of steam-powered automobiles. A year earlier, the Senators had been told that long-range and economical electric cars were still far in the future, but this time, the committees were surprised to hear a vastly different story. Ayres testified that fully competitive steam automobiles could be built almost immediately. "I know of no reason," he said, "[that] at least one or two production lines might not be put up within two or three years. I realize you cannot do this overnight, but I do not see any reason for delay in getting started."

The problem, very simply, was money. Most of the steam proponents who testified were asking for some form of government support, ranging from actually subsidizing steam car development and production to instituting demonstration and testing programs. Morse pointed out that the government could at least alter its vehicle purchasing policies to include low-pollution emissions as criteria for governmental use. This, Morse argued, would act as an incentive to steam car makers and also supply a ready-made market.

Government involvement was necessary in order to develop their competitive and nonpolluting alternative to the internal combustion engine, said the steam people, because, with the exception of the Thermo Electron Corporation, whose steam work was well supported by Ford and which was not interested in automotive applications for its engine, the experimenters were severely underfinanced. The Williams brothers and R. A. Gibbs and

Thomas Hosick had made significant advances, but both teams had problems with one part of their system and both were poor. The Williams brothers, a latter-day version of the Stanley twins, had built several experimental steam cars over a fifteen-year period, having begun their research in 1936 with their father. They were the most famous and most productive of the many backyard inventors and tinkerers, but they were also probably the deepest in debt. An economics professor testified that a large amount of money was needed to get the cars into production, but that there were ways that the government could act, also using its purchasing power, to stimulate response from the private sector.

Ford and General Motors were represented at the Senate hearings. They seemed to be there to downgrade steam, to claim that the problems that afflicted F. E. and F. O. Stanley were still with us, and even worse, that the problems that the Stanleys had solved—such as eliminating the possibility of boiler explosions—were also still with us. As if they had prepared beforehand, each company spokesman took a different tack. The Ford man said that considering a drastic change to steam was not really necessary since the auto companies would be able to reduce emissions on the internal combustion powered cars. The General Motors spokesman devoted his time to criticizing the viability of steam. He cited the "real safety hazard" of the boilers and, during questioning, said that "historically, steam generators and steam boilers have always caused trouble." He also spoke of the size of the steam system, the problems with freezing, lubrication, and auxiliary power, and the slow start-up time. He sounded as if he were back in the horseless carriage days describing the disadvantages of a Stanley Steamer, but he was speaking seriously in 1968, a powerful man speaking for a powerful company. He put the steam advocates on the defensive, where they are likely to stay, as John Maga of the California Air Resources Board has said, "until they've been out on the road for a couple of years and people have had a chance to see how they perform in everyday driving situations."

The stand of the auto companies is in keeping with their record on other challenges. In the mid-1950s, Detroit claimed that it could not curb emissions from its vehicles, until devices made by non-automotive firms showed that it was possible. Now, in order to win industry backing, steam evidently must prove itself independently as a satisfactory alternative to the internal combustion engine—or even as a significantly better one. Steam advocates are confident that the job can be done. They believe that, taking into account steam's low-emission characteristics, its superiority is a provable fact. And some declare that steam is superior on its own merits as a power source, even waiving its low-emission advantage.

One type of steam unit consists, very basically, of a burner, a boiler (also called a generator), the engine itself, and a condenser. The burner heats water (or another liquid) in the boiler to produce vapor. The standard fuel in most modern steam systems is kerosene, but almost anything can be used—diesel oil, number one or number two oil, or even paint thinner. The steam generator usually has a single coil of tubing of very small diameter (the so-called monotube boiler minimizes water leakage and boiler size). To move the car, the engine valve is opened, letting steam into the engine block, where it performs similarly to the fuel-air mixture in an internal combustion engine. The steam expands in the cylinders and pushes the pistons forward. This motion—again like that of an internal combustion engine—is transmitted to the crankshaft, which transfers the power to the wheels. Since the steam is formed outside the engine block, the first two strokes of the internal combustion engine's four-stroke cycle can be avoided, but the final two strokes—expansion of the steam pushing the piston forward and the backward motion of the piston driving the steam out of the cylinder—correspond to the final two strokes.

After the piston pushes the steam out of the cylinder, it is sent through the condenser where it is recooled into water. The water is then recirculated to the feedwater tank, where it is ready to be heated and vaporized again. In this way, the process is continuous, and several thousand miles can be driven on one filling of the water tank. Most advanced systems use a very small quantity of water in the boiler, which makes possible faster start-ups as well as more efficient use of water.

The steam system, as we have seen, produces practically no harmful emissions through the exhaust because in it a far more complete combustion takes place than in the internal combustion engine. The fuel is burned outside the engine continuously at atmospheric pressures. In the gas engine, combustion—an explosion, really—takes place inside the cylinders at very high pressures, resulting in incomplete combustion and in the emission of large quantities of poisonous pollutants.

The steam system's continuous combustion at atmospheric pressures also has "no stringent requirements on 'octane' ratings," according to Dr. Ayres, so there is "no need for tetraethyl lead in the fuel." With fuel free of the lead needed by most gas cars for better performance, there is obviously no lead to be emitted into the atmosphere.

The steam car uses its fuel during cruising and acceleration; while idling and decelerating, it uses little fuel and emits no pollutants. A properly tuned steam engine would emit only carbon dioxide and water vapor, which are harmless.

Steam's proponents are convinced of its other advantages. Donald Johnson, president of General Steam Corporation at Newport Beach, California, who was the developer of that company's unique and powerful steam engine, says that his research was not at all motivated by emission characteristics. "We were originally just looking for a power source suitable for driving a low-wing aircraft, and after three years of research on all kinds of power systems—turbines, Rankine, internal combustion, everything—we found that the Rankine-cycle steam engine could do the best job in terms of power-to-weight ratio, torque, and noise."[7]

Morse, whose company is interested in nonautomotive applications for steam engines, is impressed with steam's ability to use any of a number of liquid fuels which give more BTUs (British Thermal Units, a measure of energy) for less cost than either gasoline or diesel fuel. "Furthermore," he said at the Senate hearings, "the capital investment in terms of refinery costs—and the oil and gasoline industry is a heavy capital industry—will be considerably less for the production of fuels for an external combustion boiler as opposed to [those intended for] use with an internal combustion gasoline or diesel engine."

Perhaps the main other advantages of steam are its torque characteristics and its quiet operation. The steam engine is very powerful at low speeds and has high torque at all speeds which is handy when climbing hills or starting from a cold start. Gasoline driven engines have torque corresponding to engine speed—that is, they have high torque only when running at high speed. Dr. Ayres points out that this characteristic of steam "makes it possible to eliminate the clutch and transmission which adds substantially to the complexity, weight, cost, and maintenance problems" of the internal combustion vehicle. The lack of power is especially crippling on larger vehicles, such as trucks and buses, says Ayres, where it results in a "great deal more gear changing than automobiles." Steam systems would completely eliminate transmissions and gear changing and all the problems that go with them.

The ride of a steam car is smooth and silent. The noise from a steam system is about four times less than that from an internal combustion engine. "I think the public is getting fed up with noise," Morse says, "and in the future, the noise levels will get worse." And, says Ayres, "if engine noise were eliminated, a stronger incentive might exist for undertaking measures to reduce noise from tires." Quieter and fumeless cars would mean, at the least, that it would no longer be a nightmare to live near a highway.

Another favorable attribute of steam is its efficiency of performance. More of the power from the steam engine would go directly to the rear wheels. "It is estimated that 40 per cent of the engine power of an ordinary internal combustion engine is dissipated within the power train," Ayres said at the Senate hearings, "whereas only about 10 per cent of the power of a steam engine is wasted in this manner." The so-called parasitic power losses of a standard car would, therefore, not be losses at all in a steam car. The efficiency at the rear wheels would be greater with a steam-driven system.

But how about the problems? How have the disadvantages that have historically been associated with steam been eliminated? An extensive list of problems with steam has been drawn up by Professor S. William Gouse of Carnegie-Mellon University, who, after working on a Morse subpanel and testifying at the Senate hearings, has become a strong advocate of steam cars. In an article entitled "For Smog's Sake, Steam-Powered Automobiles Should Come Back," in the May–June 1968 issue of *Engineer*, Gouse wrote:

> The steam-powered automobile generally has a poor image. To it has been attributed: slow starting in all weather; freezing problems in cold weather; heavy weight; danger of boiler explosions; complicated operating characteristics; short range; poor economy; high cost; and the need to license the driver as a steam engineer.

But, he went on, "these deficiencies are indeed only apparent, stemming from the very early days of steam-powered automobiles." Gouse reiterated that "the later Stanley and, of course, the Doble steam cars were very acceptable—perhaps their biggest problems were that they were never set up for mass production and suffered from poor business practices."[8]

But even since the Doble, there have been significant improvements. The Williams brothers, by building compression in the exhaust stroke of the piston so that the pressure inside the cylinder stayed fairly high and constant, were able to increase the thermal efficiency of the steam engine considerably. Steam systems in automotive sizes now have thermal efficiencies of 20 per cent or more which is somewhat better than the thermal efficiencies of internal combustion engines in actual driving conditions.

The size and weight of modern steam systems have been substantially reduced. Now steam systems can be put into the same space as a gas-powered system and weigh a bit less. The first system developed by William P. Lear, a major industrial entrepreneur now involved in automotive steam, included a rather large but powerful (300 horsepower) engine that fit under the hood of a standard-sized passenger car, along with the burner, generator, and condensing system. The system weighs about the same as a complete system for a gas car. And, as boiler size is decreased—Morse has developed a very small and efficient boiler five times smaller than the Williams boiler—the size and weight of the system may be reduced still further.

Engine size and weight have been reduced by Johnson at General Steam Corporation. He has the cylinders—six are standard—arranged cylindrically around the axis as in a revolver. His major innovation is the cam which is used instead of a crank. His so-called barrel-engine is smaller and more powerful than conventional cylinder configurations, and Johnson has plans for making still smaller ones. On existing car engines the crankshaft carries the power from the pistons to the wheels. But Johnson's cam, a doubly-inverted, helix-shaped piece of metal, avoids large tool-up costs, as well as making for a lighter and smaller engine.

Steam systems should be able to equal or exceed the speed of a standard automobile. Fuel consumption is a bit less with steam. A steam car should make about 30 miles per gallon of kerosene or diesel oil. All advanced steam systems being considered for automotive use are closed-cycle systems—their water is recirculated, so that filling the water tank is a rare event.

"Hermetically sealed" systems such as the Thermo Electron engine make it possible to use smaller condensers since condenser efficiency is higher when all air is excluded.

Start-up time under normal conditions is down to eight or nine seconds in the General Steam system, and Lear had estimated that one system on which he was working would be able to start in twenty seconds at twenty degrees below zero. According to Gouse, "improved burners and combustion chambers, more sophisticated steam-generator design and higher-service materials make for virtually no time-delay at start-up." Freezing and lubrication problems are generally handled by using soluble oil mixed in with the water, although other approaches have been tried. Both Lear and Johnson have experimented with oil in their systems. Whether the oil actually serves to keep the system corrosion-free is something that, Morse says, "we will not know for a couple of years." But it does seem to have eliminated freezing as an important difficulty.

Many steam developers are interested in alternate working fluids, that is, using some liquid besides water for vaporization. This might increase thermal efficiency and—since liquids are being considered that have lower freezing points than water—would also eliminate freezing. Freon has been tried, but it has been found to decompose at temperatures below the level at which a vapor engine operates efficiently. Lear has said that he has a "million dollars to pay for a working fluid that would bring about 40 per cent thermal efficiency," but it might be a while before that liquid is found.

The cost and complexity of steam systems have also declined significantly since the Stanley Steamer days. Controls have been developed that can bring the boiler temperature and pressure close to predetermined levels. The fewer moving parts of a steam system make it a less complex piece of machinery. The cost of parts should be less than for the gas engine once the steamers are made on assembly lines. Because the parts of both systems are comparable—pistons, cylinders, crankcase, and valves—there should not be a great difference in price. Lear has estimated that his first-year models would cost about $500 more than a comparable i-c driven car, but, after that, mass production should bring down the cost.

Steam now has the potential, it seems, to be fully competitive with the internal combustion engine. And its advantages make it, its advocates claim, "the best possible power source that is feasible at the present time."

Chapter Five

The Steam People

Ambler, Pennsylvania, is a typical suburban community, perhaps a bit more quaint, a little less affluent than most. It is a "bedroom" town, filled with commuters who fight the traffic every day into Philadelphia. But in the early part of 1968, the traffic was moving the other way. News reporters, magazine writers, legislators, businessmen, automotive experts, TV crews, and many others came from all areas of the country to see "the car" and to talk with Calvin and Charles, the Williams brothers, who had one of the few modern steam cars in existence. As steam began to be hailed in many quarters as the answer to automotive air pollution, more and more people wanted to see what such a vehicle could really do.

The visit to the Williams home took on the aura of a pilgrimage. "First there was the jaunt in the car and the surprisingly smooth, silent ride," says Karsten Vieg, whose work in fostering legislation and testing programs in California to encourage the development of steam will be discussed in a later chapter. "Then we went out into the kitchen, and while we sat around drinking cans of Coke, the Williams brothers talked about the problems they had had through the years."

Calvin and Charles Williams had quite a story to tell. They had lived firsthand the difficulties that anyone trying to enter the automobile business on a small scale must face. They had spent thirty years tinkering with automotive steam engines and making a few experimental steam cars, but too much of that time had been spent seeking money. In 1966, a brochure they had put out with the help of Robert Lyons of the Steam Automobile Club brought ten orders for their car. They warned the prospective buyers that the cars would be extremely expensive and long in coming. But even on that basis, they were not able to produce. Where parts had been expensive and slow in delivery for individual, experimental models, the costs were even higher in orders for ten cars and the delays were also longer. At the 1968 Senate hearings on steam, Calvin Williams said that when they ordered thirty chain sprockets—used in the Williams car to drive the camshafts, three per engine— "the price jumped from $24 a sprocket to $77 a sprocket. We thought that was quite a jump. It has been that way practically on every item that we use. It seems if you want something in small quantities, it is very difficult to get a good price for it." As to the delays, "It took us a year to get castings, which we had anticipated we would get in twelve to fourteen weeks. We ran out of working capital and had to stop manufacturing operations."

As they often had done in the past, they sought more financial support. In 1957, they had driven an earlier car to Detroit for Chrysler to look at; they left some drawings and plans with the Chrysler engineers, which, Calvin Williams said at the Senate hearings, "we understand they are still studying." They had tried on several occasions to stir up government interest. They were in the same chronic quandary as other steam tinkerers around the country. They needed backing to work on and perfect their system, but until their system was perfected, the chances of getting money seemed very remote.

When the interest in steam began to surface in late 1967, the Williams brothers continued their efforts to obtain financing. They traveled around the country talking up steam, as well as entertaining guests in Ambler. They went to New York, to Dallas, to Washington, and even to the West Coast—"for Charlie Williams it was his first time west of the Mississippi," says Karsten Vieg about the brothers' appearance at the California Assembly steam hearings in Sacramento in March. They received many offers to buy their car, but none of the deals was completed. The Williams brothers drove a hard bargain. They didn't want to give up their technology without retaining a controlling interest, and, finally, when they agreed to take less than 50 per cent, they insisted that the potential buyer pay all their debts, which he refused to do.

Their isolation and financial difficulties had left the Williams brothers poorly equipped to challenge the internal combustion engine and the corporations that produced them. "Their technology," says Robert Ayres, "was ten years behind the times." People were interested in the Williams brothers, Ayres says, "simply because they had a car." William Lear, who has brought money and big business into the steam world, wrote after a visit to Ambler that the Williams car was "far from being ready for anything like production." The other backyard or basement tinkerers seemed just as hopeless. Some worked in machine shops or had completely unrelated jobs, devoting their spare time to their steam systems as a hobby. "We have a name for them," Lear wrote in a letter in late 1968, "which is not intended to be derogatory, but rather to indicate the inadequacy of their methods, their unscientific approach and their financial incapabilities— 'Kooks.' "[1]

Besides the Williams vehicle, another modern steam car existed—one built in the late 1950's by Charles Keen with some advice from Abner Doble and William Besler. Now owned by Thermal Kinetics Corporation of Rochester, New York, that car is also not very advanced. According to Lear, in all of these cars and automotive steam systems "practically none of the scientific and materials progress made during the space age has been applied."[2] Even when an interesting invention was made—as was the case with the "Elliptocline" engine of R. A. Gibbs and Thomas Hosick of Greensboro, North Carolina—the tinkerers were unable to do anything with it. Since they had done very little work with boilers and lacked the money to buy anyone else's technology, the Gibbs-Hosick engine was never run for longer than a minute. A novel valve mechanism that fed the steam to eighteen paired cylinders and led to simplifications in the engine design was expected to make the engine very powerful for its small size; but, without money or testing, its capabilities could not be explored. With the burst of interest in steam in 1968, Gibbs and Hosick were looking for a buyer for their engine.

Before Lear, the state of the art seemed pretty dismal. The tinkerers were all broke or on the verge of going broke, and the well-financed companies working with steam were interested in nonautomotive applications for their systems. They were talking about putting steam engines in boats and golf carts and tractors and helicopters. Only the tinkerers—many of whom had never resigned themselves to the disappearance of steam cars (Gibbs, for instance, drives a 1901 White steamer)— were thinking about automotive applications. The well-funded firms, with their sensible managers, were more interested in putting their steam systems to whatever use seemed most profitable, and competing with Detroit did not look profitable. Thermo Electron Corporation in Waltham, Massachusetts, was one of the early financially sound organizations in the field. Founded in 1956 by two professors at MIT, George Hatsopoulos and Joseph Kaye, Thermo Electron is located on the Route 128 industrial complex that surrounds Boston. The company has conducted research and development work on various kinds of energy sources. Through both industrial and government funding, it has become fairly successful, employing some 175 people, about 40 of whom are graduate engineers and scientists. Theodore Johnson, the company's vice-president, said at the 1968 Senate steam hearings that Thermo Electron's annual sales are around $4 million. It is a sound operation, but not the kind to take on a billion-dollar industry.

Thermo Electron first grew interested in steam in 1963. The company was then under contract to the Army to develop an electric power generator for military use. Silence was a prerequisite for such a system, and someone at Thermo Electron was familiar with the low noise characteristics of steam engines. As Johnson said at the 1968 Senate hearings, the company first looked at steam when a "staff member suggested that a small steam engine generator might fulfill military requirements." Thermo Electron therefore sent some of its technical staff to a nearby steam expert, Professor Joseph Keenan at MIT. They asked him why steam had faded away as a power source. What had made people turn to the internal combustion engine? Keenan said that many of the reasons were nontechnical, as has been discussed in an earlier chapter. But, he said, steam had been displaced for three major reasons—the large size and weight of the engine system necessitated by poor methods of heat transfer, problems with lubricating oils that contaminated the water and led to corrosion of the system, and failure of the system to recirculate the water completely, making necessary constant refilling. These difficulties had been greatly reduced for automotive steam engines—Doble's car, for instance, was guilty of none of these failings—but a small, technically advanced steam engine still faced these problems. With money available, Thermo Electron's engineers set to work trying to solve them.

Since the project began, Thermo Electron has built several small, experimental steam engines, none over three horsepower. The engineers in Waltham devised a system of internal valving somewhat like the system worked on by the Williams brothers that helped to raise the thermal efficiency of the engine. The Thermo Electron system uses a much smaller boiler, having minimized the length of the boiler tubing and the amount of fluid needed to run the system. The system is hermetically sealed so that water loss is practically eliminated, making refilling unnecessary. Installed in a car, such a hermetically sealed system would have to be refilled only after several thousand miles, or about once every six months, to replace losses due to diffusion of the water.

Thermo Electron continues development of its steam systems, but will not be producing steam engines for automotive use—at least not in the near future. The company submitted a bid with Ford to make design studies of steam cars for the National Center for Air Pollution Control in the Department of Health, Education, and Welfare. In June 1969, the National Center awarded the contract to Thermo Electron over four other bidders. If the designs prove promising, the company could build a prototype steam car for the government, but it is still not considering production of cars or of automotive-sized engines. If and when Ford and the other large auto companies decide to make steam cars, then Thermo Electron will be involved—most likely through the technology that it has developed during the past five or six years. Johnson feels that "steam cars will only be produced by the large auto companies, not by a small research-oriented firm like ours," although he believes that automotive steam engines are technically feasible. With Ford's money, however, it is impossible for Thermo Electron to talk about producing steam cars. Johnson hopes to use Ford's production help to develop his company's engines for small, nonautomotive uses—power generators, lawn mowers, boats, golf carts, snowmobiles, where, he says, "silent operation, multifuel capabilities, and freedom from maintenance are perceived by the consumer as desirable features."

For automotive application, Johnson says that the efficiency would be much better with a working fluid other than water. At Waltham, he says, they are experimenting with other possible fluids that would lubricate the engine and not decompose at the temperatures normally encountered there. This has been one of the main difficulties with freon as a working fluid.

Wallace Minto in Sarasota, Florida, has experimented

with freon vapor engine systems but so far appears not to have completely solved the difficulties of decomposition. He has used various additives to keep the freon together at automotive temperatures, but it is difficult to say how successful he has been—since beginning his work three years ago, Minto has been secretive about his developments.

Aside from the decomposition problems, however, Minto has developed sophisticated engine systems. Two of his vapor engines are being tested by the Dallas Transit System in a program funded by the Department of Transportation. Minto also talks about possible auto production in the future but has refused to spell out the details. Many experts, including Dr. Ayres, remain wary of Minto's engine, reserving judgment until the results of the Dallas tests are in, sometime this year (1970).

Clear across the continent, in Newport Beach, California, General Steam Corporation has a policy like Thermo Electron's. For that company, too, money is available but not on the astronomical scale required by car-making. Donald Johnson, head of General Steam, says, "We don't want to buck the auto companies; we'd rather use them as our ally and work with them." R. G. Smith, the company's vice-president, says, "We just don't have the money or the desire to take on the auto companies. We can be a lot more successful using our system in other applications." Yet one of their engines, along with one of Lear's, is to be tested by the California Highway Patrol. Like Lear, GSC will furnish its own car. The California Assembly had originally prevailed upon General Motors to support the program, but neither Lear nor General Steam was interested in General Motors financing. Donald Johnson and Smith also talk about possible development of a racing car, so that they may be more interested in the automotive market than they admit. The company plans to "go into producing those applications that offer the greatest possibility of success," and, should the automotive market look promising, they could possibly enter it.

General Steam's Johnson is a very productive inventor, and has some talented engineers working with him. Before he teamed with Smith in 1964, he had been a backyard tinkerer like the Williams brothers. Never having gone to college, Johnson nevertheless had worked as research scientist for Union Carbide before he decided to go out on his own. Smith, an avid car fancier who once took a crack at race car driving, attends to the business end of the partnership and has found substantial private funding for his company. They are now located in two large buildings in Newport Beach, each with enough space to produce significant numbers of parts and entire systems. But they were not always that well off.

Smith says that he first heard about Johnson after he returned from New Zealand, where he had been doing missionary work for the Mormon Church. There he had met and made friends with Phil Campbell, who now is a General Steam Corporation manager. "I got a call from Phil not too long after we got back," Smith recalls. "He told me that I just had to come out to Arizona. He had met Don, and they had started talking about Don's work, and Phil became very impressed. Don was mainly talking about the principles involved in his work, the thermodynamic principles involved, and Phil thought that he had something."

After several calls from Campbell, Smith says, "I grabbed my tape recorder and went out to see what Phil was yelling about. After talking with Don for several hours, I thought he was onto something very significant, but I wasn't skilled enough technically to know for sure. So I took my tape out to Caltech and asked some professors there if what Don had told me made sense." Smith says that the Caltech people were favorably impressed with Johnson's ideas about engines and how to improve the efficiencies of steam engines, and so Smith went to work with him.

They took a few years to get settled, locating for a time in a small town on the side of a mountain in Utah. They later moved to Mesa, Arizona, where they stayed until the end of 1967, when they left for California and changed their name from Controlled Steam Dynamics, which they had been called originally, to Thermodynamics Systems. Recently they took their present name, General Steam Corporation. After struggling for three years, Smith obtained financing, and the company is now on a firm financial footing. But that footing is not enough to give them the incentive to take on Detroit. "The auto industry is the toughest nut to crack," Smith says. "If the auto companies were to say that steam is the thing, then steam would make sense. But not until then."

Still, both Johnson and Smith feel that their engines will be able to perform in an automobile as well as, if not better than, an internal combustion engine; if the Highway Patrol program is successful, perhaps General Steam Corporation will reconsider producing engines for automotive use. They would like to set up some kind of licensing arrangement, by which they would supply the technology and somebody else would do the production and the advertising. For now, they have begun to produce prototype steam systems for a wide variety of applications, with helicopter or light aircraft applications being the ones most considered. Wherever a market exists, Smith says, they will produce engines for it. They themselves will not go into the automobile business, but, should somebody or some company want to buy their engines for automobile production, they would be willing to make a deal.

Although they have been working on a variety of different engines, the one that would be suitable for automotive use—the one that will most likely be used in the Highway Patrol program—is fired by two generators, each rated at 75 horsepower. The engine has a high range of 500 revolutions per minute (rpm). At 480 rpm, Johnson says, the engine develops 150 horsepower. The system is closed cycle—there is no loss of working fluid—and can start up in ten seconds. It can be placed in the engine area of a standard car and weighs a bit less than a standard internal combustion model. A small turbine engine provides auxiliary power for the radio, air conditioning, power control systems, and the same turbine in other sizes may have other applications as well. Johnson is thinking about using the turbine in golf carts and power alternators. It is extremely quiet—Johnson says that you can stand two feet away from it and not even know it is operating—which is a valuable quality for other uses. Johnson believes that his cam-type engine—the crank of the shaft axis is replaced by a cam, making the engine smaller and lighter than a standard engine—is far superior to other power sources.

Back in Massachusetts, Richard Morse also is trying to find the best area to break into the steam engine world. Unlike Johnson, Morse was drawn to steam because of its low-emission characteristics. It was Morse's panel which propelled the whole movement toward steam; it was Morse's testimony at the Senate hearings that helped bring the government to take steam seriously, and it was Morse who blasted the auto companies for what he termed their "ostrich posture" in the field of emission control at the 1968 meeting of the Society of Automotive

Engineers (SAE). Morse warned the auto industry at
that meeting that they should be cautious in criticizing
steam because, if they ignored steam long enough, it was
just possible that companies outside the auto industry
might take the lead in steam car development. Morse
drew an analogy between the auto industry and the tex-
tile industry, where, he said, "Everyone knew that cotton
and wool were unquestionably the 'ultimate,' the only
thing, and it took the chemical industry to prove otherwise." He gave other examples of development work on a
product that had been done outside of the particular industry that produces that product, and concluded, "The
time is ripe for innovation in the auto industry—or, in
view of the above examples, perhaps we should say the
time is ripe for automotive innovation in other industries."[3]

Morse helped found and now heads Energy Systems,
Incorporated, which will in the near future begin to produce steam engines. "We think that the way to get into
this business is to have a lot of muscle," he says, and he
has made arrangements to combine with Mobil Oil Company and an engine tooling company. "Then we will have
capital, management, and tooling production," he says of
this plan, which was "well down the line" in early 1969.
Being backed by a tooling company means that parts
would not be a problem, and the oil company would
supply much needed capital. The Williams brothers and
the other tinkerers never had either of these advantages.
After more studies, Morse says "We'll see where the best
place to enter the market will be. But we will definitely
be looking for nonautomotive applications. It's simply
too tough to enter the auto field at this time."

Morse talks now of truck and bus applications. One of
his company's first actions after its formation in late 1967
was to submit a proposal to the Department of Housing

and Urban Development to replace the diesel engines in city buses with steam. The large diesel-driven buses, Morse says, "are about the ugliest things I've ever seen. They're noisy and they smell, besides contributing to pollution." Morse's study found that steam would be a practicable alternative, and HUD came close to funding a testing program. (The Department of Transportation— DOT—has set up a program to test steam-powered buses in San Francisco and freon-powered buses in Dallas. Both programs will be discussed in more detail below.)

To take part in an infant industry is nothing new for Morse. As president of the National Research Corporation in Cambridge, Massachusetts, for many years, Morse played a part in developing industrial applications for the mass dehydration of penicillin and large-scale vacuum melting of metals and alloys. He also helped organize the Minute Maid Corporation, a pioneer in the production of frozen citrus concentrate. Morse believes that his latest enterprise is potentially just as promising as the others.

He has enlisted the services of "four or five experienced Ph.D. types," as he puts it, and has a plant in Newton, Massachusetts, which, he points out, is "right across the river from where the Stanley brothers had their first plant." Morse's company plans to build engines and has bought a good deal of technology. The most important purchase, Morse says, was a license for a rotary valve mechanism originally developed by Robert Black in Texas several years ago. With such a mechanism, Morse says, it is possible to convert existing two-cycle internal combustion engines into steam engines and get, as a result, very high efficiencies as well as a continuously variable torque. Morse's company has been running a complete system with this kind of engine since late 1968 with encouraging results. "We are convinced," he says, "that we can compete with the internal combustion engine in thermal efficiency and can beat it in both size and weight of the engine, as well as torque, noise, and emissions."

Much of the research being done by Morse's engineers is aimed at reducing the size of the boiler. Morse claims that they have been able to build a boiler that is extremely small and very efficient—"probably a fifth the size of anything we know about." If a boiler were only 75 per cent efficient, Morse reported in the study for HUD, it could still be used in a steam system that would be economically and technically feasible in a large city bus. This means that the conversion could be made with a relatively large boiler. But Morse now claims 90 per cent efficiency for his boiler, meaning that a much smaller boiler could be used which would be more efficient. The effect would be an even shorter start-up time and more power at lower speeds. Morse's work in reducing boiler size indicates that there are still ways to improve steam and shows, as does the work at Waltham, Sarasota, and Newport Beach, what financial support can do toward developing steam as an advantageous alternative to the internal combustion engine.

Among other nonautomotive applications, Morse is thinking of steam power for tractors, boats, buses, and trucks. He is seeking to establish his company's financial independence and has said that he is not interested in government financing or in financing or support from the auto companies. General Motors, he says, offered to supply him with a large quantity of free diesel engines that his engineers could convert to steam, but he refused. "They try to stick their nose in everyone's operation," he says, "but we are trying to stay clear of them."

The steam world has changed drastically in the short

time since steam cars were hailed as the answer to automotive air pollution. "Two years ago," Morse says, "everybody was laughing at the whole business." But not now. The big money that has been long in coming is being pumped into the steam-engine world, and it is going into well-managed and well-organized companies.

The new steam experimenters can no longer be called "kooks," although the backyard inventors who championed steam over the years are mostly being left behind. The companies described in this chapter will be heard from in the future. Right now, however, none of them seems to have what R. G. Smith of General Steam has called the "astronomical amounts of money needed to produce cars." And none seems willing, or especially eager, to take on Detroit.

Chapter Six

Lear

Steam cars have always attracted a strange breed of man.
Because of the steamer's outsider status in the society,
the men who have created, developed, and built steam
cars have invariably been out of the ordinary. Some have
had truly inventive minds, turning to steam because it
challenged their technical ingenuity—like Leon Serpollet
and Donald Johnson. Some have been tinkerers with an
almost fanatical devotion to steam—like the Stanley
twins and the Williams brothers. Others have been en-
terprising businessmen who have found in steam a way

to turn a good profit but who have had neither the passion nor the inventiveness of a Serpollet or a Stanley. The producers of the White car at the turn of the century and Richard Morse today might fit into this category.

But invention, devotion, and business sense go only so far, even when they are effectively combined. A fourth ingredient—money—must be included in the mix as well, something that few devotees of steam have had in any sizeable quantity. With money, so the story goes, Serpollet would have put steam on French roads forever, the Stanleys would have overwhelmed Henry Ford, and Charlie and Calvin Williams would have ruled the highways for the past twenty years, with Ambler supplanting Detroit as the auto capital of the world.

But before falling too quickly into fantasy, we must remember that Serpollet wasted most of his money and was an unpersuasive businessman; the Stanleys insisted their cars be handmade, screened their customers meticulously, and refused to advertise; and the Williams brothers never seemed to get much good out of the funds they did manage to raise. In short, money alone has not been the whole problem. It had to be used with a grand vision and a willingness, even an eagerness, to take enormous risks. After a long wait, steam cars have finally attracted a man with both money and verve.

William P. Lear is putting his considerable business experience and his money into the production of low-emission powerplants right now. At a former Air Force base ten miles north of Reno, Nevada, he is developing steam and hybrid engine systems, and, in 1971, he hopes to be producing close to 1,000 engines a day. He promises to have steam powerplants ready to test sometime in late 1970.

The multi-millionaire's arrival on the steam scene during the summer of 1968 was well-timed. For months steam advocates had been declaring that steam was the most immediate answer to the air pollution problem and that only money was needed to demonstrate it. But the right kind of money was needed, the kind of money that would scare Detroit, that would prove to the auto companies that they had a fight on their hands. Small companies, even well-funded small companies, could be bought off by the auto giants, or be persuaded to cooperate with them. Nor could the government compete with Detroit. But Lear thought he could.

"I looked around," he said in December 1968, "and saw that if somebody didn't do something, the auto industry would bury steam just like it had done before."[1]

Lear was already bringing industry to Reno in hopes of providing some diversification for the gambling-dominated economy. Before the steam project, he had set up Titanium West to produce titanium ingots, and he also planned to produce automatic pilots for airplanes and power alternators, in addition to starting a precious metal refinery. He sees his enterprises as providing the industrial base for a future technical community in Reno that would also include the nearby Desert Research Institute and the University of Nevada.

All of this would sound fantastic if Lear had not made a name for himself as an industrial innovator in the process of accumulating a sizeable fortune. He likes to tell people how his fellow industrialists said he was crazy when he began to develop the Lear Jet, which became a very profitable undertaking. With the steam automobile he is apparently treading on even more dangerous ground, but he seems willing to accept the risk. "In twenty years," Lear says, "the internal combustion engine as we now know it will be an oddity."

In a magazine article in early 1969, less than six months after he first decided to produce automotive steam engines, Lear proclaimed of himself: "Here is one guy who has gathered together the greatest group of engineers in the country in what was once a gaming town, one guy willing to prove that by gambling $10 million on one roll of the dice he can produce a steam engine that will be the world standard of excellence. It will at the same time solve the air pollution problem. . . . Now then, if I do it, I will have solved a national community health problem and at the same time challenged the largest single industry in America, if not the world. By comparison, Nick the Greek was a piker."[2]

Lear started his legendary business career in radio and electronics, developing the Majestic radio set and operating the Majestic Radio Company without any formal technical training; he had left school after the 8th grade. He then turned to automobile radios and pioneered with Paul Galvin in the founding of Motorola, which, Lear points out, has "not exactly been a failure."[3] "Finally my interests wandered into aircraft," he has said, because "my love of aviation exceeded all other loves." He developed direction finders and radio transmitters and receivers for airplanes, and, in 1949, he was awarded the Collier Trophy by President Truman for his work on automatic pilots. While inventing devices, he was also building another company, Lear Aviation, which became Lear Siegler, a $200 million a year concern. When his fellow managers refused to back his plans for a low-cost corporate jet airplane, Lear sold out and started a new firm, Lear Jet. That was also the name of the plane—over 230 of which have already been made with no end in sight. The Lear Jet proved to be a tremendous success. Lear calls it the "most economic, fastest, highest flying, lowest cost business jet ever developed, and it is doubtful that that record will be altered for many years to come."[4]

In 1966, Lear sold his interest in Lear Jet to the Gates

Rubber Company for a healthy profit. But while he had accumulated many millions of dollars and over 100 patents through his years in business, he still felt that he had not made his mark. By 1968, after an operation on an artery near his brain and after breaking his leg getting out of his limousine, Lear was, he said, "despondent because of the lack of a challenge." The retirement to which he had been sentenced at 66 in his home in Beverly Hills, California, was empty. His life was not yet behind him. It was about then that he became interested in steam.

"My initial interest in steam for automotive purposes," Lear has said, "dates back to 1918 when I was sixteen years old and not only drove the steam cars of that day, but was somewhat of an automobile mechanic as well." He therefore studied the articles and reports on steam in 1968 as an old believer. He was interested in the non-polluting characteristics of steam cars since he was daily exposed to the smog in Los Angeles and recognized that it was getting worse. He decided to investigate steam-powered vehicles further.

He made, he says, a "cursory but subsequently thorough examination of the state of the art." He visited the tinkerers and the small businesses. "The thoroughness of my investigation," he says, "took me all over the country and where I couldn't go, I sent agents to make investigations, and it was always the same." The work was meager, underfinanced, haphazard—and Lear seemed to have found a cure for his despondency. "The sum total of my findings," he has said, "showed that here at last was something that could be the challenge I was looking for and especially in view of the fact that the automotive industry had taken the position that steam just wasn't the answer and never would be. That made the challenge all the more stimulating!"[5]

Lear chose a large chunk of land north of Reno on which to turn his vision into reality. He has had workmen furiously reconverting old buildings and constructing new ones since he moved in during the summer of 1968. During 1969 he added 600,000 square feet of new plant space, and he plans to have 3,000 people on the payroll by the end of 1970.

Lear's plans do not stop with steam cars. He is changing Reno itself. His car and his projects are talked about as much as the gambling, and, for a town that was thought to be dying, Reno has apparently begun to come to life. With Lear, new people have come to town, new jobs have opened up, and the whole place seems to consider itself a part of Lear's super-gamble.

Of all aspects of the steam project, Lear seems most eager to discuss the people he has working with him. He has, he says, "put together a group of engineers that I believe to be the best in the whole world. As a matter of fact, I have been in business for forty-five years and I can state without reservation that I have never had a group of engineers half as good. Their approach is completely modern and completely scientific and at the same time extremely ingenious."[6] His machinists are also, he says, "the best I've ever had working for me."

Initially, Lear wanted to race a steam-powered automobile in the 1969 Indianapolis 500 auto race and started building a replica of the Indianapolis track in Reno. All through the early part of 1969, he was boasting about his car, but in April, he decided not to enter the race. The car could have been ready, he said; but rains had delayed completion of the test track and, more important, Indy race officials had refused to tell him whether or not his car would be allowed to enter.

As it turned out, entering the car in the 500 became unnecessary. The racer had already served its publicity purpose. The car was built and was exhibited at several auto shows in 1969; there still is a possibility that Lear may enter it in the 1970 Indy 500, or in other races. But, as Dick Wells wrote in *Motor Trend*, "The effort expended on the race car was better applied to consumer-oriented steam-power applications."[7]

Ken Wallis, who was Lear's general manager from the inception of Lear Motors, was a strong backer of the race-car development. He had helped design and build Andy Granatelli's STP gas turbine racer that led the field for 492 miles in the 1967 Indy 500, and he also had worked on the turbine cars that Carroll Shelby wanted to enter in the 1968 race. Wallis left Lear in June 1969, and the decision to de-emphasize racing played a part in his departure. The two men separated on something less than friendly terms.

Wallis has since gone into business for himself. He now heads Steam Power Systems, Incorporated, San Diego, and is currently designing steam systems for marine uses. He has teamed up with the Sheridan-Grey Machine Company in Huntington Park, California, which gives him the tools and equipment, and will provide financial help should he become interested in production. As of now, his work is in the design stage in San Diego, but his company will be one of the four taking part in the San Francisco-Oakland steam bus testing program (to be described in the next chapter), and may be heard from in the future. According to the bus program's director, Wallis is interested in bus applications for his systems. Sheridan-Grey certainly gives him the "muscle" to be taken seriously.

Lear later felt that Wallis had led him down the wrong path. Wallis had developed the so-called delta engine which had three crankshafts arranged in a triangle with six cylinders and twelve pistons. The engine was very powerful and could be scaled up for different sizes, producing 760 horsepower for the racer and about 400 horsepower for a passenger car.

After Wallis left, Lear turned his attention to steam turbines. The delta reciprocating engine was, a Lear spokesman said, put on the back burner. The system that would go into the California Highway Patrol test vehicle in summer 1970 would be a steam turbine. Lear's engineers had concluded that the overall efficiency of the turbine would be greater than that of the reciprocating engine, and they urged Lear to give turbines a try. Production facilities were being readied in late 1969, and the first systems were expected to be produced at about the time this book is published.

It is unclear exactly how many cars Lear will produce. Originally he planned only to build the engine systems and supply them to auto companies and to auto parts shops. As people needed major adjustments on their cars, Lear hoped that they would choose to have a steam system installed. He also hoped one of the auto companies would cooperate and put the Lear system into one line of their production. Karsten Vieg remembers Lear taking this approach in October 1968. "He said that it would be stupid for him to take on Detroit," Vieg said, and Lear echoed this view to all listeners at that time. But, by early 1969, Lear was exploring the possibility of producing his own cars. Whether he thought the auto companies would be more willing to produce steamers if he himself produced them first, or whether he felt that the auto companies could never be convinced, he considered meeting Detroit head-on. He would buy the bodies from whatever company would sell them to him. "They may," he said, "have to be foreign cars."

Through 1969, however, Lear continued to shift his plans and priorities. He began to concentrate on bus applications for his system—as well as non-vehicular uses altogether. He spent a good deal of time negotiating with bus companies for testing programs, and many possible arrangements were investigated—among them, gas turbine engines. Lear had reportedly obtained some interesting experimental results. One of the Lear engineers' early designs, a Lear spokesman said in late 1969, showed encouraging possibilities regarding the elimination of the high fuel consumption that has, up to now, plagued gas turbines (for more on gas turbines, see chapter nine). In fact, throughout 1969, Lear kept broadening his field of interest. Money had become a problem, even for Lear, and he knew that he could not go into production unless he received some financial support. He seemed to want the auto companies to show interest in his work—financial interest—and was looking into all possible low-polluting power sources to try to find something that would be both marketable and profitable.

It is clear, therefore, that Lear does not want to set up a General Motors on his tract of land by the mountains north of Reno. He would like nothing more than for the auto companies to agree to a licensing arrangement by which he would supply the engine systems and the auto company the bodies. "Think what could happen to a company like American Motors if they had guts enough to be the first ones to successfully produce a steam-driven automobile in large quantities," Lear has said, "or even the Chrysler Corporation. The reason I don't mention the other two is because they have already found their position, but the opportunity should be enormous for Number 4, if not equally as great for Number 3."[8] Representatives from American Motors went out to Reno shortly after Lear began to work. "They were flabbergasted," Lear has said. "They admitted it would take Detroit two, three years to get to the point where we are now in Nevada. To say the least, they were shook."⁹

During 1969, however, Lear realized that he could not take on the auto companies, at least not singlehandedly. He said that it would cost $300 million to go into any kind of meaningful production of steam cars. And with $5 million of his own money invested in steam, he began to seek additional funds. Perhaps, by the time this book is published, Lear will have obtained some more financing. If he gets the money—and he is probably the most likely person in the steam world to get enough financing to go into production—he will be able to produce cars fairly soon. Nevertheless, his initial plans are interesting to relate and show what is possible today if massive financial support could be given to the steam-powered automobile.

Lear's plans were for a moderate-priced steam car, in the $3,000–$6,000 range. The cost of the engine system was to be about $500 more than an internal combustion system, and then, as production increased, the cost was expected to be fully competitive. A half-sized engine could be produced for use in smaller cars. Then it would be possible to market a steam car in the low-priced range; in fact, it would be possible to transform any car into a steamer, according to Lear, simply by varying the size of the boiler. The more power desired, the bigger the boiler, the more expensive the system.

In a reciprocating engine, the steam expands in the cylinders, driving pistons, which then turn the crankshaft. In a turbine, the steam, after being compressed in the generator, supplies power as it expands against rotating turbine blades. The initial Lear turbine engine was eight inches in diameter and about a foot long. Changes have occurred rapidly at Lear Motors, however, and by the time this book appears, the size of the engine may have changed drastically. Lear may even have returned to reciprocating engines. But the system produced for the California Highway Patrol should be a turbine, weighing about as much as the internal combustion system it replaces. It supplies 300 horsepower as compared to the 200 horsepower of the i-c engine previously used by California patrol cars. In a bus, the first Lear turbine system weighed considerably less than its competition. The engine, generator, condenser, and burner together weighed 1,200 pounds. Lear spokesmen claimed that the Cummins engine which is standard in most buses weighs 4,000 pounds.

Lear believes that the weight of the automotive steam system will decrease very soon. He has his engineers working on smaller and lighter turbine engines and reciprocating systems as well. In the initial cars, he planned to have a torque converter attached to the engine system which would permit the engine to power the auxiliaries. In the bus, a small turbine would handle the auxiliary power. Lear says that the total system is as advanced as possible. The control apparatus for the generator is fully mechanized so that there is always steam pressure available, and the size of the generator is steadily being reduced by Lear's engineers. The first one designed at Reno was about twice as big as the one that will go into the Highway Patrol vehicle, and Lear expects to get the size down even further as the work progresses.

Lear hopes to make his systems available to as many people as possible as soon as possible. "It is our intention," he has said, "to ultimately establish franchised installation stations and dealers who will be able to replace present engines and transmissions in older cars with our systems at a reasonable cost."[10]

Before Lear entered the scene, the only producers of steam systems for automotive use who were still in business sold their systems at a far from attractive cost. Richard Smith and Karl Peterson of Midway City, California, who together formed the Empirical Engineering Company, primarily sold smaller parts for steam hobbyists. They had also put a steam system in a Volkswagen and had offered to build engines and generators for the general public. But without the money needed for production in large quantities, they had to charge from $9,000 to $19,000 for the engine and the generator alone, the cost varying with the size of the system and the number ordered.

Lear is convinced that steam will work. He believes that he can revolutionize the automotive industry. In a few years, he says, "the gas car will only be in museums —in the Smithsonian in Washington." He also acts as his own best press agent, and if he can follow through on just half of the claims he makes, his project will be an extraordinary success. His power system, he says, has completely solved all the problems that have historically been associated with steam. It will be able to start in 20 seconds at 20 degrees below zero. With warmer air outside, or after use, it will start even quicker. Initially, Lear used soluble oil mixed with the water to help deal with freezing and lubrication problems. "It was pretty hard," Lear says, "to find a working fluid that would stay together at 1,500 degrees and also not freeze at temperatures that would be encountered in this country. All the heavy molecular fluids that have low freezing points, like freon, come apart at high temperatures. But with our fluid there is no decomposition at any point. We showed it to some of the best chemists in the country and nobody believed that it could be done. But we've done it." Lear's scientists continue to look for alternative working fluids that would have higher thermal efficiencies than water. In 1969 they were enthusiastic about the possibilities for heavy water. Using the turbine helped eliminate lubrication problems, since there are only two bearings to keep oiled. Normal anti-freeze can solve freezing difficulties, but, before production begins, Lear hopes to have developed a year-round fluid that will not need anti-freeze.

The turbine engine, ideally, can be smaller and lighter than a reciprocating engine and needs less refilling and refueling. The main problem with steam turbines in the past was the high cost needed to scale down for automotive sizes, but Lear feels that his systems will be able to compete successfully with the internal combustion systems. On that, of course, we will have to wait and see. But the inherent advantages of a steam turbine—higher efficiency due to the higher temperatures that can be used, better torque and power characteristics, less fuel and working fluid—make it an attractive possibility. Lear is the first to consider assembly-line production of steam turbines, and, if he has been able to solve the cost problems as he claims, he should have a most marketable product.

The reciprocating engines may be produced in the future, probably in smaller sizes. Lear's present concentration on turbines does not rule them out—the half-size engines that he hopes to have available for smaller cars could very well be reciprocating piston engines.

Lear has gone further than the tinkerers. He has "utilized computers and materials that are available in the space age to build a small, reliable engine."[11] He expects his cars to be fully competitive with the internal combustion cars in addition to having the advantages of low emissions, silent operation, and more power at low speeds. His engine is planned to get as good mileage on a gallon of kerosene as the internal combustion engine gets on a gallon of gasoline. And Lear is quick to point out that the oil—either in the form of kerosene or diesel oil—

will be less costly for the oil companies to produce than gasoline.

Lear, by late 1969, was still in the research and development stage. He was, however, seriously thinking about production and was trying to get financial support to make production possible. Whether or not he goes into production depends in part upon the American people. If pressure on behalf of a solution to the automotive air pollution problem continues strong, Lear and the work he has done until now stand ready to make a significant contribution. Some efforts—by the California legislature and by the federal government—have helped him, but such efforts so far have not been enough. With additional financing and continuing public support for nonpolluting automobiles, Lear may still bring his plans to fruition.

His dream was to build steam-powered passenger cars and build the racer to advertise them. The plans have changed somewhat, but the enthusiasm has not waned. Lear is seriously in the steam car business, and his accomplishments have been very much his own. He has even shied away from calling his cars "steamers" to avoid the image of a 1905 antique buggy, for Lear's car promises to be of this age. He proudly proclaims that the only thing wrong with steam was that the technology and the development methods of the space age—as well as the production techniques—had not been applied to steam. Now he has changed all that. In the process, he may also have started the machinery going that will ultimately revolutionize the automobile industry in this country.

Chapter Seven

California's Activity

The California state capitol sits, surrounded by palm trees, in the middle of a park in downtown Sacramento. With the possible exception of the brand-new airport several miles out of town, the capitol is more impressive than anything else in smoggy Sacramento. What has been accomplished inside the building for air pollution control has been even more impressive. California's legislation setting up control procedures and emission standards has served as models for the country. The California legislature was the first—before any other state and before the federal Congress—to set up an agency to control the emissions from motor vehicles. The California legislature has sought to tighten its emission standards beyond those established nationally or in any other state. It must be hoped that California's groundbreaking 1968 legislation, setting up a steam-car testing program and encouraging the development of extremely low-polluting vehicles by assuring a market for such vehicles, will similarly serve as models for the other state and the federal legislatures to follow.

Only part of the explanation for California's pioneering in smog control lies in the severity of its air pollution. Indeed, some of the large eastern cities have topped Los Angeles and San Francisco in surveys of the nation's smoggiest urban centers. Nevertheless, more of a public furor has been raised about the smog in California than anywhere else, and the California legislature can justly claim to be responding to the voters' demands.

Possibly a more important factor is the organization of the legislature itself. Many people who have been to Sacramento claim that the operation there is more advanced than on Capitol Hill in Washington. Staff men proudly proclaim that theirs is the finest legislature in the world —including all national legislatures. Whatever comparisons can be made, California's legislature is undoubtedly well-equipped in both staff and procedures. It certainly is one of the nation's richest. But money alone cannot do its work without a guiding hand. In California, the key man, most people on both sides of the aisle will admit, was Jesse Unruh, who served as Speaker of the Assembly from 1961 to 1968. In a paper presented in July 1968 at the State Legislator's Seminar in Key Biscayne, Florida, Arthur Bolton, former director of the Assembly Office of Research, indicated the reasons for the body's power and effectiveness. "It is generally known," Bolton said, "that

California has the best staffed legislature in the nation. For many years we have had about one hundred budget analysts, attorneys, and auditors serving both houses of the legislature." He went on to say that "Since 1961, when Jesse M. Unruh assumed the speakership of the California State Assembly, the Assembly has further developed its staff services to expand the capability of individual legislators and legislative committees."[1]

Each assemblyman has a secretary and a full-time administrative assistant in his district office, so that he can keep in touch with his constituents. The twenty-two committees of the Assembly all have professional staff people who have been trained in the committee's area of concern. Bolton says that these consultants are not political appointees. "Most committee consultants," he said, "have survived changes of committee chairmen—even when the new chairman represents a different political party than his predecessor."[2] In 1965, a separate nine-man research staff was set up for the caucus of the minority party so that minority assemblymen could originate their own legislation. Bolton claims that the "competition in ideas" made possible by the minority research staff "has helped to raise the level of partisan debate."[3]

Probably the most significant innovation took place in February 1967 when the Assembly set up its Office of Research, which Bolton headed until the elections of 1968 sent him over to the minority research staff. But even if the Office has not been able to overcome all the problems of partisanship inherent in a political organization, it has brought a new degree of professionalization into a state legislature. It was set up to provide the kind of research that could not come from one or another committee. The assemblymen had seen the value of people with different points of view working together. California's medical care program, for example, was formulated by staff members of the Public Health, Revenue and Taxation, Finance and Insurance, Ways and Means, and Social Welfare Committees. "As this type of cooperation developed," Carlos Bee, the Assembly's Speaker pro tem, said in late 1967, "we learned the value of bringing together various skillful people with different professional backgrounds—people with no agency loyalties or dogmas to defend."[4] The Assembly Office of Research was therefore established with sixteen professional staff members to look at the state's needs from all vantage points. They would be free to conduct extensive investigations and to work as long on a subject as they thought it required. They would not be tied to any particular legislator or committee.

One of the first studies undertaken by the Office of Research was on smog. It was headed by Karsten Vieg, who, along with Joan Reid, spent most of 1967 and 1968 investigating California's air pollution problem and the attempts that had been made to solve it. The goal was to draft legislation that could improve the situation. "Fifteen months ago," Vieg said in October 1968, "I knew next to nothing about smog, other than that we had it and it was bad. I was just like any other concerned Californian." When he began to investigate, he was distressed with what he discovered. He found that 90 per cent of the air pollution in Los Angeles, San Diego, and Sacramento was contributed by motor vehicles—even though the state smog agencies had been trying to control emissions since 1960.

Vieg decided that the auto companies were the main impediment to progress. "Any lasting solution to exhaust emission or evaporation loss control involves engine and fuel redesign by Detroit," Vieg wrote in a memorandum to Assemblyman John F. Foran in October 1967. "Redesign is expensive, and every year it can be delayed is money saved as far as Detroit is concerned. Thus we have a situation in which the people who are least inclined to help us with our problem are the people to whom we *must* turn for help."[5]

Vieg felt—and he became more convinced after a trip to Detroit with several legislators in early 1968—that the answer to the problem would not come by playing along with the auto-makers. California, he thought, would have to initiate the change on its own. He pointed out in his memorandum to Foran that the California Department of Public Health had set up an emission standard for oxides of nitrogen, "but since Detroit says it cannot develop a system to control it," he wrote, "we have no controls."[6]

The need for control was, Vieg found, growing more urgent. "There is mounting evidence," he wrote to Foran, "of a direct relationship between vehicular pollution and the creation, aggravation, and acceleration of respiratory and lung disease." He found, as well, that the current standards were not doing the job. "Los Angeles and San Francisco are already 'protected' by California's exhaust emission standards; standards which are not yet required by the federal government," he wrote. "Yet within the last two months both cities had severe smog conditions —Los Angeles the worst in eleven years."[7]

Before any legislation had been proposed, Vieg set up exploratory hearings before the Assembly Transportation and Commerce Committee, which Foran headed. One of the key witnesses was Louis Fuller, the control officer for the Los Angeles Air Pollution Control District. Fuller had worked hard for over a decade to control the stationary sources of air pollution in Los Angeles, but he felt that his work went for naught as long as the state floundered in controlling vehicular emissions. He was especially critical of the policy that allowed some cars to exceed the state emission standards so long as the average emissions from all new cars met the standards.

The hearings, and Vieg's extensive investigation, led to two important pieces of legislation, both introduced by Foran in January 1968. One bill, AB (Assembly Bill) 357—later to be known as the Pure Air Act of 1968—called for the most stringent emission standards ever recommended for motor vehicles. As Foran put it, the bill was the "strongest smog control measure ever to appear before this or any other legislative body."[8] Rather than leaving the job of setting specific emission standards to the state control agencies, AB 357 included the standards directly in the legislation. The concept of averaging was greatly tightened, although problems of testing made it impossible to eliminate it completely. There would still be some cars that would not meet the standards, but the number would be greatly reduced.

Under the Federal Air Quality Act of 1967, California needed a special waiver from the Secretary of Health, Education, and Welfare to establish emission standards more stringent than the federal requirements. Before Foran's bill was voted upon, the Assembly set up a nine-member Technical Advisory Panel to study the standards in AB 357. The panel, with a member each from the oil industry, the engine industry, a county smog control agency, and a state smog control agency, and five members from California universities, was to review the bill so that its technical requirements could not be brought into question.

The panel held six meetings—one with representatives of the auto companies—and reported its conclusions in April 1968. The standards in AB 357, including one for oxides of nitrogen, were, the panel said, technically feasible, although they warned that "if the standards are universally applied, some makes and models of cars will not be permitted to be sold."[9] With their recommendations in hand, the bill was passed and was signed by the governor in July.

At the same time, another bill became law—the former AB 356, which had also originated in Vieg's investigation of the smog situation in California. He felt that the provisions in AB 357, even though they would get progressively tougher through 1974, would still not be able to solve the problem. He thought that alternatives to the internal combustion engine must be pursued. The *Road Test* article in late 1967 had alerted him to steam, but he and the California legislature had heard more on the subject from William Lipman.

Lipman was the director of the California legislature's office in Washington. His job was to keep the state legislature in touch with key people and key ideas in the nation's capitol. In late 1967, Lipman met Robert Ayres and they discussed Ayres' forthcoming report that would speak so favorably about steam. Lipman and Vieg were becoming interested in steam cars, and they investigated the possibilities. They visited the Williams brothers and other steam tinkerers. After the Technical Advisory Panel met with the auto-makers in Detroit, Lipman reported, "We found that (1) they [the auto companies] weren't interested in steam; (2) there was some interest in electrics, and (3) all possibilities of 'tinkering' with the ICE [internal combustion engine] really didn't help. We concluded that Detroit was committed to the wrong approach: (1) whatever Detroit does to the ICE can easily be undone by private owners or dealers; and (2) there is no technology which will enable Detroit to produce an ICE that will simultaneously reduce unburned hydrocarbon, carbon monoxide, and nitrogen oxide emissions."[10]

Vieg had drafted AB 356 for Foran even before he,

Lipman, and the legislators had visited the auto-makers and the steam advocates. It was Vieg's way of having the California legislature lead, rather than follow, the auto companies. The bill stipulated that if low-emission vehicles were made in large enough quantities and the costs were not prohibitive, at least 25 per cent of the vehicles purchased by the state should be such low-emission vehicles. Vieg believed that this would be the way to eliminate air pollution—by encouraging, through the state's purchasing power, the development of a new kind of automobile engine.

Vieg has said that the old men of smog control in California—principally A. J. Haagen-Smit and John Maga, the chairman and executive officer of the state Air Resources Board—were not so hopeful about the possible benefits of AB 356. "Publicly they spoke in favor of it," he says, "but privately they were doubtful. Their main interest was getting 357 passed." Since Lear has come on the scene, Maga has become somewhat more favorably disposed toward steam, but Haagen-Smit remains skeptical. "I believe that the present automobile will be with us for a long time to come," he says. "The auto industry will see to it that the emissions will be below a competitor, such as the steam car." And, he has pointed out, "with any new system, the performance of the present-day car has to be matched, and the performance was developed over many years."[11]

But Vieg and Lipman were not to be dissuaded. They sought ways to make steam cars respectable. "Each member of the Assembly," says Vieg with a smile, "mysteriously received a copy of the *Road Test* steam article in a plain brown wrapper." Vieg and Lipman also set up hearings before Foran's committee in March 1968. "The hearings," says Vieg, "were supposed to be on all alternate forms of automotive power, but, as it turned out,

steam dominated." Lipman brought the Williams brothers to the west coast for the first time, and he also invited
Robert Lyons and Samuel Miner of the Steam Automobile Club to testify. Richard Smith and Karl Peterson,
two steam tinkerers from Midway City in Orange
County, came up to Sacramento. The Williams brothers
ran their movie—also shown in Washington at the Senate
hearings in May—which had shots of their passenger car,
as well as of their engine system powering a bus and a
boat. "They were the stars of the hearings," says Vieg.
"The committee was really impressed, and they asked us
what we could do to get steam cars on the road." The
testimony had been the usual early 1968 line about
steam. The proponents said that they had the technology
to eliminate smog, but they needed money.

The pivotal scene took place in Vieg's apartment that
evening. He and Lipman were talking, Vieg recalls, and
"Bill said that it would be a great idea, since we had all
these steam people together, to try to talk to them in-
formally. That way, we thought that we could find out a
little better what we could do and what they really
wanted." By then it was the dinner hour. "We called up
every restaurant in Sacramento and finally located them
all. We asked them to come over to my apartment for a
drink."

"When we got them all together," Vieg remembers,
"we put it to them very bluntly that the California legislature was willing to do all it could to eliminate the smog
problem." He and Lipman asked the steam advocates if
AB 356 was the kind of legislation that could help them.
"They said it was a step in the right direction, but that
what they really needed was a chance to get a modern
steam car on the road and tested." Lipman and Vieg had
originally specified in their investigation that any alternative forms of automotive power to be considered would

have to be acceptable for use by the California Highway Patrol. Vieg says that this criterion was used because the California Highway Patrol is one of the country's most respected and the best trained. "We felt that if the Highway Patrol would test a steam vehicle, then it would be a prestigious test." Vieg asked the steam advocates if one of their engines could successfully operate a California Highway Patrol vehicle, "and Cal Williams said that steam could do that and it would be able to pass the test."

The next day, Vieg, Lipman, Calvin Williams, and a representative from the Highway Patrol met in Vieg's office. The CHP representative recommended that Foran send a memorandum to H. W. Sullivan, the Highway Patrol's commissioner. On March 19, Foran did so, outlining the testing program that had been formulated in Vieg's apartment. At that time, the Williams brothers seemed to be the only possible suppliers of the engines to be tested. The Highway Patrol, Foran suggested, should conduct a one-year testing program on one to six cars powered by Williams engines. The program would not cost the CHP anything, Foran said; the cost could either be borne by the state or by some outside source. Williams estimated that the cost of the program would come to about $20,000 per vehicle tested.

Commissioner Sullivan replied. "I have read with some excitement your suggestion that this Department participate in the testing of approximately six prototype steam cars," he wrote. "Certainly in this day of constant search for new methodology to handle some of our growing problems, operational research of this type can furnish many of the answers."[12]

Meanwhile, Lipman and Vieg were looking for possible financing for the project. Lipman wrote to industrial firms, magazines, foundations, and consulted with federal officials. Nobody was interested. Vieg approached

Frank Lanterman, an assemblyman from La Canada, California. "Lanterman's brother drives one of the few Dobles left in existence," Vieg explained, "and Lanterman himself is an auto engineer and a steam buff." Vieg asked Lanterman if the state should supply the money for the program. According to Vieg, "Lanterman said, 'State, hell! Why not GM? They've been telling us steam cars won't work. Maybe they can spend a little to test the cars.'" General Motors sent representatives out to Sacramento to talk with Lanterman and Vieg, and on May 20, the day that the Assembly passed ACR (Assembly Concurrent Resolution) 111 authorizing the program, GM agreed to underwrite it. General Motors would supply up to six Oldsmobile chassis without the engine systems and also offered to pay the installation and operating expenses for the program. The company was putting up $120,000.

The resolution passed the Senate in July and by August the Highway Patrol was sending out requests-for-proposals (RFP's) to potential engine suppliers. By then, the Williams brothers no longer had the field to themselves; in fact, they were unable to meet the CHP specifications and did not submit a proposal. The bidders' conference in September attracted a great variety of other people, however, some of whom were merely interested spectators. Howard Hughes sent representatives, which led to speculation that Hughes was going into steam cars. "We all expected him to," Ayres has said. "He was the most obvious one." Several other large, non-automotive corporations were represented at the meeting. Ling-Temco-Vought of Dallas, one of the nation's largest conglomerates, had people there. For months there was speculation that LTV would enter the steam arena. "The LTV lobbyist in Sacramento was taking me to lunch quite often during the summer and fall," Vieg says, "and

I couldn't understand it. Then, a bit later, I found out that LTV was interested in buying the Williams car."

When the bids were all received in October, however, neither LTV nor Hughes had sent in proposals. Lear, Smith and Petersen, Johnson at General Steam Corporation, Wallace Minto of Sarasota, Florida, and Berry Foster of Redondo Beach were the only bidders. R. A. Kridler, the Deputy Commissioner of the CHP, announced, "We anticipate signing a contract with the successful vendor in two weeks," after the proposals had been "studied to ascertain that they comply with our specifications."[13]

It turned out to be more complex than that. The proposals turned out to be far different from what had been asked for in the RFP's. "We received one reply," says Inspector D. S. Leuthje, assistant to the CHP chief of staff and director of the testing program, "that just said, 'Yes, we can meet all the specifications.' We were unable to choose between engines." Some of the applicants felt unable to make the top speed that the CHP asked for and others could not provide the engine in the time required. Commissioner Sullivan wrote at the time, "The Department also received other communications that indicated our specifications were too tightly drawn. It was pointed out that they precluded submission by other interested persons and were overly restrictive." A second Request for Proposals was written to provide, according to Sullivan, "a clear understanding of what the Department is seeking, what items are subject to negotiation, and which are specific requirements."[14]

Leuthje blamed the mix-up on a "definite lack of communication." The original RFP had been vague, he felt, and had not given the CHP the opportunity to judge fairly which engine would do the best job. "We wanted to find out, as best we could, if there was any individual who could comply with what the legislature wanted," Leuthje said. There had been criticism of the original specifications which required that the steam-powered car should be able to go 130 mph for a distance of twenty-five miles "without slacking the speed or making any unusual adjustments."[15] Leuthje defended such specifications, however, and retained them in the second RFP. "We incorporated our Class A patrol vehicle specifications in the RFP," he says. "That was, we felt, what the legislature had intended."

After the second set of proposals was sent to the CHP and studied, Leuthje recommended that the Patrol test one car driven by a Lear engine and one driven by a General Steam Corporation unit. He had been impressed by both operations, and felt—as did the legislature, Foran said, in a letter to Leuthje—that, if two engine makers seemed equally qualified, both should participate in the program. The initial testing is expected to begin during the summer of 1970, and if the cars measure up to the CHP specifications, they will be tested for a year, driven as if they were regular patrol cars. It is interesting that Lear and General Steam Corporation have refused GM's support, and will buy their own bodies and pay for their own installation. For the slight amount of money that was involved, they felt that it was not worth getting involved in any way with General Motors. Besides, if GM had funded the program, all test results would have become public property, including installation and production information, which Lear, for one, was not anxious to disclose.

First results should be coming out of the program in the coming months. If the steam cars perform well, most steam advocates feel that the days left to the internal combustion engine will be few indeed. "The true significance," Lipman says, "is to dramatize and conclusively demonstrate the existence of a different technology as a real alternative to present automotive propulsion. . . . If such alternatives can meet the CHP requirements, they can meet all other modern-day requirements."[16]

One possible result of California's activity has already been realized—Lear has entered the field. Foran said in May 1968 that he thought it "possible that this experimental program could trigger the development of steam cars on a mass transportation basis."[17] Lipman agrees: "If the car is certified for state use, pursuant to AB 356, our Department of General Services must buy some for our state fleet. More important, the automotive avant garde, well represented in our state, will probably become customers for personal, racing, and other uses. A successful CHP test would probably also lead truck and transit operators to give ECE [external combustion engines] a try."[18]

Transit companies may turn to steam for other reasons. In February 1969, the Department of Transportation announced that it was funding two testing programs— one in Oakland and San Francisco and one in Dallas—to test buses powered by external combustion engines on normal city routes.

The California program was worked out by Vieg and Lipman, but it was initiated by officials in Washington. Vieg asked the transit authorities of all the major cities in California if they would like to participate in such a program. San Francisco and Oakland agreed. "We will do some pretesting for three months," says Lipman, "and then for nine months give the buses a test on three of the toughest areas in San Francisco. All we want to do is demonstrate that the technology already exists."

The operation of the program has been turned over to the Scientific Analysis Corporation (SAC) of San Francisco; Ayres has been retained as an advisor. In late September 1969, eleven applications were reviewed by SAC and Ayres with the help of a special advisory panel chaired by Gouse, who testified at the Senate steam hearings in 1968. The panel included Maga of the Air Resources Board, Miner of the Steam Automobile Club, James Dooley, who had taken part in McCulloch's experiments with steam in the 1950's, and four other experts in the field. The panel selected four companies for the testing program—Lear Motors, General Steam Corporation, Steam Power Systems, Wallis's new company, and a small Berkeley engineering-consulting firm headed by William Brobeck, who had worked with Doble in the 1930's and had later been chief engineer at the Lawrence Radiation Laboratory. Soon after the initial decision was made, however, General Steam quit the program, choosing to concentrate on other aspects of steam propulsion, and was replaced by Paxve, Incorporated, of Newport Beach, California. The brains behind that company is Doug Paxton, who has been working on a unique vapor-powered system (not using water as the working fluid) for the past twenty years, recently with significant financial support. By late 1969, none of the four selected systems were operable but all expected to be ready within a year.

Besides the technological delays, the bus program has also had financial difficulties. Gouse's advisory panel told SAC that the initial $450,000 grant from the Transportation Department, later supplemented by an additional grant of $300,000, would not be sufficient. A third request was formulated, and, at this writing (January 1970), that request for slightly over $1 million was still pending. Nevertheless, those involved with the Oakland–San Francisco program feel certain that the testing will be able to begin by early 1971.[19]

The Dallas program involves LTV, Wallace Minto, and the Dallas Transit System. LTV officials, who selected

Minto's engine, were impressed with the freon system. How well it operates will be demonstrated, they hope, in the Dallas program. "We spent six months investigating every external combustion engine we could find—at least a dozen—in the United States, Europe, and Australia," LTV's public information director, Jim Roth, has said. "We finally decided to go with Mr. Minto's engine because it was the best around."[20] LTV—actually LTV Aerospace Corporation, a subsidiary of the parent company—is building the buses that will carry Minto's engines. They will also handle the installation. LTV was expected to have the buses ready by the fall of 1969, and then to give them over to the Dallas Transit System for a year of testing—six months of pretesting and six months out on the road carrying passengers. But there have been problems with the installation and, at the beginning of 1970 the contract with the Transportation Department was still unsigned.

Chapter Eight

The Role of the Federal Government

"In a perfectly operating free competitive market system," Robert Ayres said at the 1968 Senate hearings on steam cars, "there would be no 'pollution' problem. The market's 'invisible hand' would—subject to some qualifications I need not discuss here—operate to produce maximum social welfare. This is one of the basic postulates we make about the operation of our economy."

The government has taken a long time to find out that this postulate is invalid. Government pollution authorities have had to learn the hard way what they should have done. To the credit of many officials, all manner of steps are now being taken to do something about our air, but only after numerous mistakes have been made, and numerous assumptions have been disproved. Washington maintained that state and local governments should have ultimate control over pollution abatement programs. Until recently, it was the government view that private industry should research and develop new ways of eliminating emissions. Nobody could have known in 1955 which was the best way to proceed; and in all fairness, it must be said that government pollution authorities have tried to learn from the mistakes of the past, as well as from the successes of others, particularly the California legislature and Air Resources Board. But the government has moved slowly, and often it has moved in ill-advised directions.

Recent evidence indicates that government pollution control officials may be more helpful in the future than they have been in the past. They are finally beginning to feel the sense of urgency about pollution control. Most important, the government at long last is taking an aggressive stance in the development of alternate power sources, notably steam cars.

In 1955, the United States Congress passed its first piece of pollution control legislation. Interestingly enough, that first bill was part of a water pollution control act. In the hearings on the legislation, air pollution was not thought important enough for separate hearings —it was considered only as a part of the larger set of hearings on water pollution. Officially amended—and in actuality severely overhauled—four times since then (in 1963, 1965, 1966, and 1967), the act set up a pollution control division in the Public Health Service of the Department of Health, Education, and Welfare. The division was to support research on air pollution and provide technical assistance to states and cities. "This legislation established the policy," a 1968 HEW report explained, "which continues in effect, that State and local governments have a fundamental responsibility for dealing with community air pollution problems, and further, that the Federal Government has an obligation to provide leadership and support."[1]

By 1963, the air pollution problem had grown far more critical. The legislation on the books was not doing the job. A special subcommittee of the Public Works Committee on air and water pollution—which has since become a permanent subcommittee—held hearings which strongly indicated that the government should be doing more. S. Smith Griswold, the executive officer of the Los Angeles Air Pollution Control District, declared that large amounts of money were needed, and, as he had in 1955, Griswold urged increased federal support. Los Angeles, he said, had spent over $45 million to improve its air quality, which was "more than the Federal Government has spent since the inception of its program in air pollution." Griswold said of his district's expenditures, "I feel that it has been well justified; it had to be done. We are not complaining about doing it, but we feel that from now on we would like to work with the Federal Government to get into the increased ramifications of this very complicated subject rather than having the responsibility of doing it ourselves."[2]

Other witnesses agreed with Griswold. Washington was urged to become more involved in pollution abatement. As the HEW report explained, "It was becoming clear that progress toward a better understanding of the problem was not being matched by real progress toward better control, primarily because most state and local governments were still not equipped to cope effectively with community air pollution problems."[3] The Clean Air

Act of 1963 was aimed at improving the situation. It called for increased federal funding of research, particularly in the area of motor vehicle pollution, and also for more federal supervision of interstate control programs. But the problem has, thus far, failed of solution, even though legislation has become increasingly stronger.

In 1965, amendments to the Clean Air Act empowered the HEW Secretary to establish national emission standards for motor vehicles, patterned after the California example. John Gardner, then Secretary of HEW, issued standards effective for 1968-model cars, and the standards for 1970 model cars are tighter still. But the auto company lobbyists were influential in keeping the emission standards from being set even lower. The auto companies do the research and have the technology, says a HEW official, and "we can't change the standards until we have the technology."[4] In emission standards, he says, the government has not followed the lead of California, where, "the standards are set first, and then they wait for the technology." Recently, after a great deal of soul-searching and some public demand, Washington has decided that it must help provide the technology.

With the Air Quality Act of 1967, the HEW Secretary was given greater control. Ultimate control was put in the hands of the federal officials. A greatly expanded research effort was called for. HEW was required to provide "detailed information on techniques for preventing and controlling air pollution," to quote the 1968 HEW report. "Provided with this information," the report continues, "states are then expected to develop ambient air quality standards and plans for implementing these standards." HEW was handed the authority to review and approve the state's plans, and, "if a state's efforts prove inadequate, the Secretary is empowered to initiate abatement action."[5] The extent of ultimate federal control has been made clear during 1969 hearings, at which the HEW Secretary, Robert Finch, had the power to decide whether California could have automotive emission requirements lower than the federal standards. The necessity for California to ask federal approval for a program stronger than the federal one seems to be an unfortunate bureaucratic difficulty brought on by the 1967 Air Quality Act. (HEW later approved the California program.)

In the years since 1955, then, Washington has expanded its efforts. There is now within HEW a National Center for Air Pollution Control, and there are pollution control branches or agencies within the Departments of Transportation, Housing and Urban Development, Commerce, and Interior as well. There has been more research, more experimentation, more development, and more testing programs. Still, the existing legislation has not proved sufficient.

It is, of course, important to realize that the government has not acted monolithically toward the problem of pollution control, although most of the departments and agencies have followed similar philosophies. The Senate Subcommittee on air and water pollution headed by Senator Edmund Muskie of Maine, and the Commerce Committee headed by Senator Warren Magnuson of Washington, have been instrumental in pushing the federal program further than it otherwise might have gone. Much of the credit for the success of federal air pollution control programs goes to Senator Muskie and his committee staff for drafting legislation and holding extensive hearings. As Bryce Nelson wrote in *Science*, after passage of the Air Quality Act of 1967, "The approval of Senator Edmund S. Muskie (D. Maine) is almost essential for any legislation on pollution. . . . It is obvious that no congressman swings the weight that Muskie does on pollution matters. His influence even carries over to the House of Representatives, partly because few Representatives seem to be as concerned about air pollution as Muskie is."[6]

However, officials of the executive branch have not been equally active. Often, they have urged the legislative branch to tone down its demands to have the government do what they felt should be left to private industry. Again, there have been times when the two branches of government played against each other altogether. The case of government support for electric and steam cars is a good example.

The legislators—primarily Muskie and Magnuson—became interested in alternate forms of automotive power in late 1966. As mentioned in chapter four, four bills were introduced which would have earmarked several million dollars toward support of electric car research and development. In opening the electric car hearings in March 1967, Magnuson said, "It seems to me that two groups should serve as the initial market to stimulate this development. One is the electric power industry which stands to profit from the increased use of electricity. The other is the Government. The imaginative and selective purchase of prototype electrics by the Federal Government may reward new breakthroughs in design, and help assume the burden of privately financed research and development."[7]

It was clear, however, that the Administration's pollution authorities were willing to give private industry more time to carry out the research on its own. "The legislation was opposed by all automobile and oil industry witnesses," Lawrence Lessing wrote in *Fortune*. "More unexpectedly, all the Administration witnesses (except those from the Federal Power Commission) also registered their opposition, on the premise that private industry be given a chance to perform."[8] The government testimony was probably one of the prime reasons that the bills were never reported out of committee.

Alan Boyd, then Secretary of Transportation, was the first Administration witness to testify. "We believe," he said, "that research on electric vehicles is first and foremost a responsibility of private industry. The Federal Government has a responsibility to assure that the products of industry meet standards of safety for public use, but not to determine what those products shall be."[9] Dean W. Coston, deputy undersecretary of HEW, agreed with Boyd, as did J. Herbert Hollomon of the Commerce Department and Stewart Udall, Secretary of the Interior. As Udall put it, "I think the administration view at this point is that industry ought to bear the main burden, and that we are not convinced that Federal input into the research effort on electrically powered automobiles would be advantageous at this time."[10]

Coston and Hollomon asked the senators to wait until the Morse panel on electric cars had completed its study and presented its report. They told the senators that the report would be ready by early fall, and that it would be unwise to pass any legislation before it was issued. This approach did not delight the senators. Senator Philip Hart of Michigan was speaking for several other members of the two committees when he said to Coston: "This may come as comfortable news to some of those that Senator Griffin [also of Michigan] and I represent, but it is sort of disappointing news to me. I would have hoped that we would have information available long before next year on which this committee prudently could act to improve the level of the atmosphere."[11]

The wait was not an unexpected one, in fact, but the lack of communication between the executive and legislative branches—the legislative in the dark about the

Morse panel until the legislation was drafted and the hearings were set—made for a great deal of wasted time, much counterproductive work, and embarrassment on both sides. The real issue—cleaning up the air—seemed to have been forgotten.

Fortunately, both sides apparently learned their lesson. When Senators Muskie and Magnuson held hearings on steam cars in 1968, there were no administration witnesses to testify and embarrass themselves, but no legislation had been drafted before the hearings were held. Like the hearings held in Sacramento in March, the Senate hearings in May were exploratory in nature. They were conducted with an eye toward possible legislation, rather than to judge legislation already proposed.

The steam hearings resulted from numerous letters from steam proponents to Senators Muskie and Magnuson, whose interest had been aroused by the Morse report's favorable comments on steam. Particularly influential was consumer crusader Ralph Nader, who had helped publicize steam cars early in 1968 and who wrote a long, persuasive letter to the two senators, pointing out the need for hearings. As they evolved, the hearings centered around ways of involving the federal government in the development of steam-powered automobiles. Steam advocates urged the government to subsidize research and development work, and some even wanted the government to help stimulate the production of such vehicles. "To be blunt," Ayres told the senators, "I think the time has come for the Federal Government to create another new industry in competition with entrenched and intransigent existing interests. . . . It is not inconceivable that the Government—Federal or State—could create, by direct or indirect means, a new industry in this field." He mentioned similar things done by the government in other areas. "The nuclear power industry," he said, "was essentially created by acts of government. This has hurt the interests of coal miners and coal mine owners, but on the whole it has probably been in the national interest—not least, because it provides cities with some means of reducing their air pollution problems." Ayres also mentioned the government-inspired Comsat Corporation which develops communications satellites, and which is "directly contrary to the interests of the largest company of all—AT&T."

Only two or three years earlier, the mere suggestion that the government go into the automobile business would have been laughed at or ignored, but in 1968 Ayres was heard respectfully because, by then, practically everything else had been tried without any great success.

There are, of course, deep-seated historical reasons for the government not to enter the auto industry, as well as modern-day political considerations. "I think the philosophical issue that is involved here," Transportation Secretary Boyd had said at the electric car hearings a year earlier, "is whether or not the public policy issue is of sufficient immediate importance that the Government should take over the active direction of research as opposed to the historical approach of the competitive, free enterprise, profit-oriented industry of our country undertaking the initiative."[12] Senator Russell Long of Louisiana at the same hearings in a more informal way said, "Well now, the thought that occurs to me is that the automobile companies are doing research in this field, and doing a good job of it. . . ." And he said later talking about the free enterprise system, "It has been that way for—I forget exactly when, but since the second year of George Washington's term, it has been that way, so your reaction to it is that the free enterprise system got us here. We are the most mobile nation on earth, and . . . the problem is being solved just by industry going on ahead and doing the job."[13]

The auto companies are one of the chief components of our economic system; they have developed without government intervention. They have been the models for our economy, showing what free enterprise can do. The automobile has become the symbol of American affluence and the companies that make cars are inextricably intwined in the American way of life.

By the 1960's, however, there were signs of disenchantment with the automobile companies. The role of cars in accidents and air pollution began to be explored, and the auto companies showed themselves to be somewhat less than enthusiastic about making their products safer or cleaner to operate. The reverence and respect that the public felt for the auto companies came back to haunt the car makers. It did not sit well when the auto companies sounded more concerned about money and power than with the safety of their products.

Something more than regulation was necessary. A study report by the Commerce Committee staff that grew out of the hearings was published in mid-1969: it recommended increased government action, and legislation, at that point, was forthcoming to require the government to use its purchasing power—somewhat like California's Assembly Bill 356—to foster the development of steam cars and other low-polluting vehicles.

Lloyd D. Orr, an economics professor at Indiana University, discussed the problem in a somewhat different context at the Senate hearings. He said that the chances appeared remote that a privately-financed company could compete with Detroit. The costs were too high and the problems of setting up dealers and going into production on a scale large enough for meaningful competition were too great. Orr also said that the chances of Detroit voluntarily building safer or less-polluting vehicles were also remote. "The problem," he told the senators, "is that where economic power is concentrated in a few hands, the discipline of the classical competitive market is absent. . . . The large corporations with vast resources and research facilities do not usually initiate fundamental innovations which compete with their existing capacity. Why should they? In the absence of sufficient competitive pressure, the large successful business protects what it has achieved. The risks and uncertainties of innovation are for the hungry man who has much to gain and relatively little to lose."

Some "hungry men" have shown their faces since Orr said these words. Lear and the other potential steam car makers do hope to compete with Detroit. But there is still a role for Washington to play. Steam car makers will not put the government pollution control people out of business. Instead they will make their job easier. By now, presumably, the government need not worry about being accused of "intervening" in the auto industry; the notion that the "free enterprise" system alone will do the job has been pretty well discredited. The government can, and hopefully will, spread information about the advantages of steam and electric cars, and it can purchase them itself. It can also make it easier for steam car makers to succeed by providing tax incentives and tax benefits for them and their customers.

One of the recommendations of the Morse panel on electrically-powered vehicles was that HEW launch a $60-million, five-year program "to support innovative developments useful in the establishment of future emission standards."[14] It urged that the money be spent on research and development of special purpose and general purpose cars powered by sources other than the internal combustion engine, as well as for continued research on i-c engines and emission control devices for them. An increased effort was called for, the panel said, because all federal pollution control programs needed to be improved: "Authority and responsibility for air pollution research and control activities have not been established at an organizational level within the Federal Government consistent with the magnitude and importance of the problem."[15]

Since the report was issued in late 1967, several departments and agencies have examined their programs. The National Center for Air Pollution Control expanded its research efforts. The Center became interested in coordinating a research program on steam cars, but in late 1968, Dr. Kay Jones, the assistant to the Center's associate director for control technology research and development, asserted that the program had been waiting over six months for the go-ahead from the Bureau of the Budget. But the envisioned program was itself a slow and drawn-out one. "Our program," Jones said, "would be to sit down and design a Rankine-cycle propulsion system. Then after studying a series of designs, we would decide which design was the most technically feasible, and then we would start to try to solve the problems in designs."

In June 1969, the Center awarded a twelve-month contract to Thermo Electron, teamed up with Ford. Selected from five final bidders—including Continental Motors Corporation, LTV, Battelle Institute, and Andy Granatelli's STP Corporation (in combination with Planning Research Corporation of Los Angeles)—Thermo Electron was charged with completing conceptual design studies of a steam-powered automobile by June 1970. The initial award was for approximately $170,000.

If all goes well, Jones hopes that a prototype steam car might be ready in three or four years. Dr. John Middleton, the Center's director, thinks a prototype will be ready by 1975. With other cars already in production, such an approach might now be unnecessary. Jones expects their research to become a "multi-million dollar" project, but the money now might be better spent on testing vehicles and building cars rather than in making designs. California seems to have found the most direct approach, which the Department of Transportation also likes—getting the cars on the road and testing them to determine how well they actually work.

The interest shown by the Transportation Department reflected a basic change in attitude from that expressed by Boyd in 1967. Even in early 1968, when Karsten Vieg and William Lipman were searching for financing for the California Highway Patrol testing program, the Department of Transportation had turned deaf ears along with other government agencies. California Assemblyman John F. Foran wrote to Senators Muskie and Magnuson at the time of the Senate hearings on steam cars, "Based on our contacts, present federal research and development effort in this area can only be classified as leisurely. The federal interest in steam, compared to federal interest in internal combustion engines or electric power, is low-pressure, to say the least. California's approach under ACR 111 [the resolution that set up the Highway Patrol program] may seem unsophisticated to some federal investigators; but, because we are very interested in results, we will chance that."[16]

At last, however, it was the Department of Transportation and not California which initiated the steam-bus testing programs for Dallas and San Francisco–Oakland. Morse has suggested that the Post Office Department test steam-powered trucks and that other federal agencies test additional applications of steam power. "The federal government should work for demonstration purposes," Morse says, "and the Congress should certainly legislate to include low-pollution characteristics as purchasing criteria."

After the Senate hearings, staff members of the Commerce Committee set to work to study the steam technology more intensively. In their report, *The Search for a Low Emission Vehicle*, published in March 1969, they recommended that legislation along the lines of California's AB 356 be introduced in Congress. The report called for increased testing programs on steam vehicles to demonstrate their performance characteristics, and also urged HEW to accelerate its steam-car research program.

In November 1969, the kind of legislation proposed by the report was introduced in Congress. Magnuson and Muskie were joined by Senator Henry Jackson of Washington in sponsoring the Senate bill, and forty-five Congressmen, led by Paul McCloskey of California and Thomas Foley of Washington, introduced a similar bill in the House of Representatives. As Morse and others had suggested, the bills would require the government's General Services Administration to purchase low-pollution vehicles (such as steam, electric, or turbine cars) if the costs of those vehicles were not more than 25 per cent greater than the cost for a comparable gas-driven vehicle.

If passed, such legislation could be a real boon to a prospective steam vehicle producer. In 1968–69, the government bought 46,430 buses, trucks, and ambulances, and 15,706 automobiles, spending a total of $154 million. The program proposed in the legislation would therefore cost the government at most $35 million a year. "This is a small price to pay for curbing the air pollution epidemic and preserving a life-sustaining environment," Magnuson said in introducing the legislation.[17]

In recent months, the President himself has talked about the need to control air pollution. As of this writing, however, there has been little but talk. The government should expand its testing programs, the Congress should pass the legislation that Magnuson has proposed, and all branches of government should do whatever they can to get low-pollution, steam-powered automobiles on the roads. "The automobile companies appear unwilling or incapable of transcending the internal combustion engine;" Magnuson said in November, "They have announced that the main battle against automobile air pollution has been won, but this is not the case."[18]

The government must do all it can to persuade, or, ultimately, to force the auto companies to switch to steam or other low-polluting power sources. The present government view seems to be that testing, research, and, possibly, selective purchasing are the principal contributions that it can make. And, indeed, it has taken Washington a long time to come to even this tentative conclusion. Such programs do serve a purpose, but they should be vastly expanded. A massive federal effort is called for, because, if such an effort is not forthcoming, the quality of our air will not only not get better, it will very probably deteriorate still further in the years ahead. The government must do all it can and spend as much money as is necessary to get steam-powered vehicles on the road as soon as possible. As John Lindsay said recently, "Either we move now to preserve our environment or we will find very soon that our environment no longer has the capacity to preserve us."

Chapter Nine

The Other Alternatives

Toward the end of summer 1968, two electrically-powered automobiles set out from opposite ends of the country, each aiming to reach the other side first. One car, a converted Volkswagen Microbus, had been developed by students from the California Institute of Technology (Caltech) in Pasadena; the other, a Chevrolet Corvair, had been converted to electricity by students from the Massachusetts Institute of Technology (MIT) in Cambridge. Teams of students from both schools did the driving.

The cars had trouble along the way. The Caltech motor burned out in Arizona and the drivers had to wait 23 hours for another motor to be flown out to them. Both cars were pushed, pulled, towed, and tugged for many miles during the trip because of recharging problems and other difficulties. The MIT entry conked out completely 130 miles from Pasadena and crossed the finish line only with the help of a tow truck. Although the eastern car thus reached its destination first, the Caltech car was officially declared the "winner" of the race because it had covered a greater amount of distance on its own power.

The cars took nine days to cross the country—some 210 hours of driving. The batteries took up an inordinate amount of space in both entries—almost all of the trunk and backseat area. The race mainly demonstrated that electric cars, as long-range vehicles, still have serious difficulties to overcome. Unfortunately, it didn't show what electric cars are capable of doing. Very few advocates of electric cars would claim that such vehicles could replace the gas-driven car completely or now serve as a workable alternative. The argument is that electric cars have great potential for limited range uses and that, in the near future, sometime in the late 1970's or the 1980's, the electric could be an efficient urban and even suburban automobile.

Like steam vehicles, electric cars were around in the horseless carriage days. In 1899, more electrics were produced in this country (1,575 of them) than gas cars (only 936). But, it is interesting to note, there were more steam cars produced than either of the others (1,681 steamers were built in 1899). Like steamers, though, electrics had all but faded away by the Depression. Some of the reasons for their demise were non-technical—poor production and marketing techniques—but unlike the always technically-competitive steamers, the electrics suffered from problems of short range, low speed, and long periods of recharging. It didn't help, of course, that electric cars were more expensive or that they were never really mass-produced. Perhaps the history of the electric would have been altered had Henry Ford and Thomas Edison gone through with their plans to mass-produce electric cars in 1915. Nevertheless, the electric did disappear, a victim of its technical limitations, which remain unsolved to this day.

Largely nontechnical reasons must be sought, however, for the failure of electric delivery trucks to catch on; economic and social factors explain in part why other short-range uses of the battery vehicle were not exploited. In England, battery-powered delivery trucks and smaller town vehicles have been produced in fairly large numbers since cars and trucks were first made. Yet, aside from some industrial fork-lift trucks and golf carts, electric vehicles have been almost nonexistent in this country since the 1930's. Michael Ference, Ford's vice-president for scientific research, testified on the subject at the 1967 Senate hearings on electrically-powered vehicles, held jointly by the Commerce Committee and the subcommittee on Air and Water Pollution of the Public Works Committee. He cited the higher cost of gasoline in Europe and mentioned the differences in delivery routes in England and the United States. "Conditions in London and other major urban areas are favorable to electric vehicles," he said, "as local delivery routes are very short, with frequent stops. By contrast, conditions in the United States require the ability to cover greater distances at greater speeds. On most routes, local delivery vehicles travel at relatively high speed on urban freeways during the course of a typical day's service."[1]

Ference's testimony was supported by Horace Heyman, a former director of the Smith Delivery Company and the Battronic Truck Corporation, two producers of electric delivery trucks in England. Heyman said that the "pattern of life in England" has been of "great help to our industry." Most people there own only one car and many do not have large freezers and refrigerators in their homes which would enable them to store food as easily and conveniently as American families. "We continue to live in separate little houses rather than in apartments," Heyman continued, "which tends to spread the population, which increases the distance to shops, and makes delivery of such foodstuffs as milk and bread a necessity."[2]

Electric vehicles in England are driven by lead-acid batteries, the standard storage battery. A car powered by such a battery system has very definite limits on how fast it can go, and how far, before being recharged. The English experience, however, has shown that vehicles driven by such batteries have certain advantages in costs of operation and maintenance and can satisfy many uses. In fact, the English government seems far more responsive than the American in encouraging the production of electric cars for urban use. In this country, as Ford's Ference said later in his testimony, the emphasis is on developing batteries more powerful than the lead-acid, rather than exploiting the batteries we now have.

Superficially, statistics seem to favor a short-range electric car—60 per cent of all automotive trips in this country are shorter than five miles and over 90 per cent are under twenty miles. This might lead to the conclusion that 90 per cent of the vehicles in this country could be electrically-powered since even lead-acid batteries can drive a car for twenty miles at sufficient speed. But such figures can be notoriously misleading. Lloyd D. Orr has testified at Senate hearings that electric car advocates must be wary of misreading statistics. The fact that most automotive trips are short does not mean that electrics could take over the market. "This reasoning ignores the fact that people tend to buy automobiles that meet their peak needs of range," Orr has said. "There are often *several* short trips to be made on a single overnight battery charge, and longer trips involving intercity travel are fairly frequent." Orr therefore concludes that the "attractiveness of a commuting vehicle with lead-acid batteries is thus limited to situations where there are two or more cars per family and one can be used almost exclusively for regular short trips."[3] Even a two-car family, however, may find it convenient to be able to cover long distances at highway speeds with both.

In 1967, Ralph Nader and others declared that General Electric had developed an electric vehicle that could reach speeds of 80 miles an hour over ranges of 200 miles. They further claimed that the car could be recharged in a matter of minutes. GE's management denied both contentions; the company had then said that it had developed a "strictly experimental" electric car that could travel at speeds of 55 miles an hour and go 100 miles on a charge. In late 1968, Electric Fuel Propulsion of Ferndale, Michigan, announced that it was producing an electric car that could reach a top speed of 60 miles an hour with a range of 70 to 120 miles. The same company had donated the batteries to the Caltech VW across the country. The Electric Fuel Propulsion car, powered by lead-cobalt batteries, was probably the most advanced electric car in the country in mid-1969, but slow acceleration, long recharging periods, the large amount of space taken up by the heavy battery system, and problems with braking were difficulties still to be overcome, and the range and top speed were good only for urban and suburban driving. As one reporter said after a ride in the car, "The theory of electric power is intriguing, but the execution still has a long way to go."[4]

The performance of electric cars is determined by what are called the energy and power densities of the batteries. The energy density—the main measure of the car's range and top speed—refers to the amount of energy stored in the battery system and available to move the car. The energy density is measured in watt hours per pound (wh/lb). The power density is the principal measure of the car's ability to accelerate, to climb hills, to move against resistance. It measures the speed with which the battery system can convert the stored energy to the mechanical power necessary to drive the car. The power density is measured in watts per pound (w/lb).

In recent years scientists and engineers have looked for battery systems that would provide high energy and power densities. But other factors—cost, length of life of the battery system, and efficiency—have had to be taken into account as well. Ference of Ford has said, "It is our engineering judgment that it will be necessary to develop batteries with energy densities of 100 watt-hours per pound or better," before it is possible "to produce acceptable electric vehicles."[5] Gasoline engines and tanks of fuel, he points out, have energy densities between 600 and 1,500 watt-hours per pound.

Lead-acid batteries have energy densities of 10 to 15 wh/lb. The lead-cobalt, nickel-cadmium, silver-cadmium, and silver-zinc all have higher densities, but in none of them is the energy density high enough and would only be able to power a small road vehicle for limited range use. And it must be remembered that the faster an electric car is driven, the less distance it can travel before recharging.

The batteries so far tested in automotive applications

suffer a variety of other problems, as well. The silver batteries are very costly; it has been proposed that the silver be rented to the car-owners, but the short life of the batteries would make such a procedure impractical. The life of the silver-zinc battery rarely exceeds 100 rechargings. As the subpanel on Energy Storage and Conversion Systems of the Morse panel on electrically-powered vehicles concluded, "Present commercially available rechargeable batteries cannot provide the range *and* power to match or approach performance characteristics of vehicles propelled by the internal combustion engine."[6]

All batteries work on the principle that when two dissimilar metals (electrodes) are immersed in an active solution (electrolyte), an electrical current will flow from one to the other if a conductor is provided. The batteries mentioned above—lead-acid (electrodes of lead and lead dioxide in sulfuric acid), nickel-cadmium, and silver-zinc—have long been used for many purposes, but only in recent years, spurred by increasing recognition of the dangers of air pollution, have scientists and engineers begun to search for a battery powerful enough to drive an automobile. New batteries are being designed, each with its own problems to be solved.

Two things cloud the future of electric automobiles. First, work on other types of nonpolluting engines is proceeding rapidly and steam or gas turbine engines may be in use before a satisfactory battery can be developed. Second, two of the most promising new batteries—sodium-sulfur and lithium-chlorine—have been developed by Ford and General Motors respectively, and future work on them will be done at the discretion of those companies. Their degree of enthusiasm may be indicated by that comment by Henry Ford II cited earlier in this book—"We have a tremendous investment in facilities for engines, transmissions, and axles, and I can't see throwing these away just because the electric car doesn't emit fumes."[7]

When he left Ford for Xerox in March 1969, Dr. Jacob Goldman, who had been head of Ford's scientific laboratories, said he still believed that Ford would have a practical electric car built by 1976. "I'm still as bullish as I ever was," Goldman was quoted in *Motor Trend*, "that there is going to be a place in the market for an all-electric or some form of hybrid electric car."[8] Formidable technical problems, however, must be overcome on both experimental batteries—Ford's sodium sulfur and GM's lithium-chlorine—their high operating temperatures, for instance. But both batteries have high energy and power densities, and with intensive developmental work, might become practicable motive power sources. It is disturbing to note that both Ford and General Motors announced their battery discoveries in 1966 soon after bills were introduced in Congress calling on the government to launch a large-scale research program on electric vehicles.

Electric proponents still hope that battery cars will be built in the next few years for limited range uses. It seems unlikely, however, that batteries can supplant the gasoline-driven car in all its functions. For a full-fledged alternative of a nonsteam or vapor variety, the thinking turns to fuel cells.

Fuel cells, which are a kind of battery that can be refueled quickly and easily, were first invented in 1839. In the past decade, there has been a great deal of research and development work on them, as the Morse report notes, "more than was done over the entire previous period from their discovery." At the present time, fuel cells are complex, costly, and heavy. In some applications—such as powering rocket engines—fuel cells have already been utilized; but for vehicular uses, much engineering work remains to be done. They can undoubtedly provide substantial power and energy for an automobile. They can, the Morse subpanel reports, "provide vehicle range greater than any known battery system." But, the subpanel adds, "present fuel cell costs must be reduced by a factor of 10–100 before they can be considered practical for consumer use in automotive vehicles."[9] Considerable work is being done in this area, and it is possible that fuel-cell-powered automobiles may be available even before electric cars driven by the advanced batteries of the motor companies.

There has also been consideration of hybrid power sources—where one battery system would provide the high power density (nickel-cadmium batteries have been mentioned in this regard) and some other system, possibly a fuel cell, a steam engine, or even a gasoline engine, would provide the high energy density. Some hybrid vehicles have already been built, but construction must be greatly simplified and other serious engineering problems solved. Most of the proposed plans are very costly, but costs aside, large-scale production of hybrid power sources for automobiles seems to be a good many years away. Robert Ayres has said that the "fuel-cell battery hybrid, which in many ways is an ideal powerplant, may be a reality by 1980."[10]

Most of the research at the Chrysler Corporation for alternative forms of power has gone into gas turbine engines. Chrysler—as well as Ford, GM, and several large non-automotive firms—has been working on the gas turbine engine for many years, and has built turbine-powered passenger cars that have performed remarkably well. The turbine's problems are not limited range or limited speed, as was demonstrated by the performance of Andy Granatelli's STP turbine car in the 1967 Indianapolis 500 auto race. What is in question is whether it is

practical to power passenger automobiles with gas
turbine engines, considering their high fuel consumption
and high cost. In its summary of findings, the Morse
panel on electrically-powered vehicles wrote, "Gas turbines are reasonable alternatives to internal combustion
engines in the large sizes used in trucks, trains, and
buses, but are not now economically feasible in the
smaller units required for automobiles."

Turbines are attractive not only because of the power
that they can produce, but also because of their low
emissions. Carbon monoxide and hydrocarbon emissions
of a turbine are down to the steam-car level, and although oxides of nitrogen remain high (primarily because the combustion process takes place at high temperatures), the engine, with only one pollutant, could,
says the Morse report, "be designed to yield low nitrogen
oxide emissions."[11]

Ford plans to produce turbine-powered trucks in the
near future (sometime in the early 1970's), and so does
Chrysler. Chrysler, whose director of research, George
Huebner, has been working on turbines for automobiles
since 1945, continues to toy with the idea of turbine-
powered passenger cars. As long ago as 1962, Huebner
was honored by the American Society of Automotive Engineers for his work "in the development of the first
automotive gas turbine suitable for mass-produced passenger cars."[12]

In 1963, Chrysler conducted a fifty-car turbine program to test consumer reaction. The cars were loaned
for three months each to families selected at random
around the country. Acceleration lag (due to a slow
torque at initial acceleration) was then a problem, but
Huebner now claims to have solved it. "Nevertheless," he
says of the testing program, "203 people had the cars for
three months each, and when our market planning orga-

nization surveyed them, we discovered there were 203 people who would buy turbines if and when produced. Of course, that didn't say what volume of market there would be, but it did say that all those people were convinced—even with the deficiencies of that engine."[13]

Along with the standard turbine problems of high cost and fuel consumption, other technical knots crop up in trying to build turbines small enough for automotive use. A Ford spokesman told the California Assembly Committee on Transportation and Commerce in December 1967 that turbines operate most efficiently at full power, "a characteristic which is undesirable in vehicular applications."[14] To operate efficiently at anything less than full power, turbines become complex and correspondingly even more costly.

A gas turbine engine is an internal combustion engine, but it burns its fuel continuously as does a steam engine. The engine, in its simplest form, consists of a compressor, a combustion chamber, and a turbine. The compressor takes in air at atmospheric pressures and then compresses it. The air is next sent into the combustion chamber where it is burned with fuel at constant pressure. The burning air-fuel mixture expands in the turbine, providing the power to drive the car, and then escapes through the exhaust. A turbine is, therefore, something of a cross between internal and external combustion engines.

Most current turbine engines used in vehicular applications have a free power turbine. "This is to say," according to a report of the Battelle Institute to the National Center for Air Pollution Control, "that two mechanically independent turbine stages are used: one to drive the compressor and the other to drive the output shaft."[15] In automotive turbines a regenerative cycle is used—a heat exchanger sends the heat from the exhaust gas to the compressor. This improves efficiency but also makes the engine system heavier and bulkier. The Morse subpanel on alternate power sources called this one of the major problems of turbines. "It is estimated," they wrote, "that 100 million dollars or more have been spent in research, development, and testing of compact exhaust gas heat exchangers in the last three decades." The group cited the difficulty of "fouling that can result from dirty air and dirty combustion" which it said was "common to all heat exchangers."[16]

Some of the problems of turbine-powered cars may be solved with more effort; and some, like the costs of materials capable of withstanding the high temperatures inside the turbine, may be more difficult. A General Motors spokesman has said, "Temperatures are at least 1,750 degrees, and materials capable of working with these temperatures cost one to five dollars a pound, compared with ten cents a pound for internal combustion engine materials."[17] Any turbine-powered car is unlikely to be a low-cost one. "U. S. industry has spent an estimated several hundred million dollars in these [gas turbine] development programs," the Morse subpanel stated. "The fact that no company has committed itself to mass production of any of these power plants is a reasonably clear indication that either the gas turbine is not an attractive competitor or that much more development and testing are necessary."[18] Turbines may soon be powering trucks and possibly buses, but automotive use seems several more years away. By that time, steam cars will, hopefully, have begun to replace gas-driven vehicles and the air pollution problem will be on its way to being solved.

It is impossible at this point in time, however, to predict the power source we will have in 1980. It most certainly will have to be low-polluting, and at least as powerful as a steam or gasoline engine. Chances are, also, that it will be relatively inexpensive to produce and relatively inexpensive to maintain. Perhaps we will be able to choose the kind of power we like best. By 1980—if not years sooner—we can hope that *all* automobiles will be low- or non-polluting. Aside from that overriding consideration, the power sources that drive the cars of the future could be any of a number of currently healthy possibilities.

Chapter Ten

Some Conclusions

The steam car—or any other low-polluting vehicle—will not, of course, be able to solve the air pollution problem singlehandedly. Nor can it begin, in anything but a minor way, to solve the innumerable other transportation problems that must be faced in this country in the years ahead. Nevertheless, the steam car is required—more than that, it is essential—if we are to make any meaningful progress toward cleaning automotive emissions from our air while still enjoying the benefits of the private car. In this chapter I will try to put the steam car in some kind of perspective and to touch as well on other developments that must take place if our future transportation systems are to make sense and our air is to be pollution-free.

Without the steam car, we are soon likely to find ourselves headed for disaster. The internal combustion engine, John Gardner warned as Secretary of Health, Education, and Welfare, is on a collision course with the American people. As the crisis grows ever more imminent, many more of us are agreeing with Gardner.

Cars are being produced in increasing numbers. By 1985, there will be over 150 million cars where now there are over 90 million. By even the most conservative extrapolation of current trends in both population and auto production, the present number of cars will double before the century is out. This book, I hope, makes clear that these cars cannot be gasoline-driven. Frank Stead, California's chief of environmental sanitation, has recommended that no gas cars be allowed in California after 1980. "It is clearly evident," Stead wrote in 1967, "that between now and 1980 the gasoline-powered car must be phased out." The "only realistic way to bring about this historic kind of changeover," he said, "is to demand it by law in the public interest; that is, to serve legal notice that after 1980 no gasoline-powered motor vehicles will be permitted to operate in California."[1] The large-scale production and wide use of steam cars would make such a stringent law unnecessary.

At the Senate steam-car hearings in 1968, many speakers—virtually all of them except representatives of the auto companies—foretold an impending crisis, a horrible contamination of our air and of our bodies if gas cars continue to be produced in ever-increasing numbers. "I have heard that the number of vehicles on our roads is expected to double by the year 2000," Congressman

Richard L. Ottinger of New York said in his statement at
those hearings. "If uncontrolled, resulting pollution levels in our cities would rise to the point where they would
become virtually uninhabitable. Driving in the country
would, of course, be much more pleasant—about like
driving in the cities today." Where air pollution alerts
occur now in our urban centers, soon—if the gas car is
not laid to rest—smog alerts and disasters will take place
anywhere, in your pleasant neighborhood and mine.

Why not ban cars altogether? Why waste time looking
for alternatives when the problem is the car itself? The
answer is perhaps unsatisfying, but nevertheless it is ac-
curate. Americans like automobiles. They have enjoyed
them since the beginning of the century, and they have
driven them ever more fervently since the end of World
War II. The estimate seems reasonable that 88 per cent
of the American people consider the private automobile
to be the "ideal mode of transportation" for all trips except business trips over 500 miles (on which they would
presumably rather fly and take advantage of corporate
expense accounts).[2] Our government builds more and
better roads every year. If all goes as planned, there will
soon be very few places in this country inaccessible by
car. Very few Americans object to the building of roads
as such. Little is intrinsically wrong with roads that offer
convenient automotive travel, but the external effects must
be taken into account. The most dangerous of these effects
is air pollution. With gas cars, the more roads we have,
the more pollution we have, even given the best emission
controls now foreseeable. The steam car, therefore, is
needed and needed quickly.

But what about the other serious social effects of our
mobile society—the congestion, the traffic jams, the lack
of breathing space? At some point, even with steamers or
turbine-driven cars, with fuel cell or battery-powered

vehicles, the number of automobiles in our urban centers will have to be curtailed. And that time is fast approaching. John Volpe, the Secretary of Transportation, has put it very bluntly. "America," he has said, "must now accept the fact that the private automobile will not forever be the absolute monarch of our core cities." New York is a glaring example of the reasons why. "In New York City," Volpe said in March 1969, "traffic moves an average of six miles per hour versus eleven miles per hour in the pushcart era of 1917." Ask anybody who lives in the city or any commuter who drives to New York to work each day from Long Island how long he gives the private automobile, and his exasperated answer will probably be in months rather than years. "I find that more and more responsible people—independent observers," Volpe says, "are questioning the survival of the automobile in the centers of our largest cities."[3]

Volpe is on record as saying that billions of dollars are needed to improve our mass transit systems. He is right. He has called for "bold, new ideas" in mass transit. "I would prefer to see the alternative of taking some people off the automobile tires if you provide good, swift, safe, economical mass transportation."[4]

Volpe admits that much of the problem has been caused by "over-emphasizing" highway building to the neglect of urban transit systems. For the richest, the most powerful nation on earth, our public transit systems are a disgrace. Many "underdeveloped" nations put us to shame. The automobile has distracted our attention. The people in the cities, most of whom cannot wield the power or the influence of the road builders or the auto companies, have been forgotten. A recent government report concluded, "Much urban transportation today is geared to the city of fifty years ago, and that city is largely obsolete today. The physical layout of most cities

—the planning, the street design, and basic service systems—was created a century or more ago."⁵

This report, entitled *Tomorrow's Transportation*, was
published in May 1968 by the Department of Housing
and Urban Development. It summarized the findings of
an eighteen-month study on urban transportation that
had been carried out on instructions from the Congress
by people in government, industry, the universities, and
the foundations. The group recommended a federal ex-
penditure of $980 million over five years in this area. The
report's authors shared the sense of urgency expressed by
Volpe in recent months, but that same feeling has not
been imparted to the Congress or the citizenry as a
whole; and it certainly has not been communicated to
private industry. But the report contained some telling
findings, as well as suggestions for future improvements.
It is apparent that something must be done about urban
transportation, and banning cars is, to say the least, not
enough.

"America's public transportation systems have been on
a treadmill since the end of World War II," the report
stated, "and they have had intensive financial difficulties
during these years. Whether public or privately owned,
few systems have been able to maintain service or
equipment." Practically no new lines have been built,
and those that have expanded have not really improved.
Most routes have remained unchanged "despite large
population shifts and important changes in land use."⁶

In all three areas of public transit—rapid rail service
(subways and elevated lines), city buses, and commuter
railroads—the service has worsened in the past twenty-
five years. Volpe has said, "If we had gone along with
mass transportation . . . at the same speed and started it
about the same time we did with the highway setup, we
wouldn't be in the mess we're in today."⁷ It will probably

be five years before new systems are operable in our urban centers, says Volpe, and "we can't wait that long for some of these things."[8] Increased attention must be directed to the problems of urban transportation in the months ahead, and a great deal of money—probably more than is now being considered—must be spent on improvements and innovations.

The state of our mass transit systems can be seen quite vividly if we look at three statistics from the HUD report —one for rapid rail systems, one for commuter railroads, and one for city buses. In 1966, there were 700 million fewer passengers using rapid rail transit systems than there had been in 1940—1.6 billion as compared to 2.3 billion. Before World War II, only New York, Chicago, Philadelphia, and Boston had subways or elevated trains. Since that time, Cleveland has added a rapid rail system, but the total number of miles covered nationwide only increased from 1,222 to 1,255—even with the addition of Cleveland's system.

The figures for commuter railroads are even more disappointing. In 1935, forty-one of our largest cities had some form of commuter railroad system, with 240 separate routes in all. By 1961, only twenty cities were covered with only eighty-three routes, and, the HUD report pointed out, "service over the remaining routes was less frequent, less reliable, and less attractive than it had ever been."[9] Since 1961, it seems fair to say that service has continued to worsen, with numerous commuter railroad lines now on the verge of bankruptcy.

The progress—or, rather, the lack of progress—in city bus service since the war is similarly depressing. The number of buses in use has increased significantly—from 35,000 in 1940 to 50,000 in 1966. The number of miles covered in bus routes has also increased—from 78,000 to 122,100. At the same time, the service has been cut. The total number of miles actually traveled by city buses in 1966 was 200 million miles less than in 1940. The vehicle-miles went down from 1.7 billion to 1.5 billion. "Even with more buses and increased route mileage," the HUD report concluded, "poorer bus service has resulted in many cases, particularly during off-peak hours and on weekends, because the buses are operating over longer routes for shorter periods of the day."[10] Merely increasing the facilities, it appears, is not enough: the service must be correspondingly improved, and urgent thought and planning must go into devising ways to improve it.

Buried in the statistics—and sometimes ignored by them—are the social problems caused by inadequate public transportation, not the least of which is an increased dependence on the private automobile. People without cars—the economically-deprived city-dwellers primarily—have had to rely on mass transit. "Nearly one-third of the urban population," the HUD report revealed, "suffer serious disadvantages from being served inadequately or not at all by the vast auto-based systems on which the nation has come to depend. These are the 'captives' left to use the transit systems, or do without."[11] And they are also those who are forced to pay increasing fares to keep the financially-starved public transit systems in operation at all. There must be some kind of freezing of fares and increasing present service facilities while other, more radical, solutions are tested and developed.

The HUD report made several proposals that could be implemented immediately. Under a section entitled "Immediate Improvements of General Application," the report listed four areas—fare collection, security, management and operations, and stations and information aids—in which action could now be taken.[12] When he spoke of the crisis in public transportation in March 1969, Secretary Volpe announced that his Department was awarding five grants, totaling $1.5 million, to the cities of Atlanta, Dallas, Denver, Seattle, and Pittsburgh. The grants were for planning studies. The test programs on steam-powered buses in Dallas and San Francisco–Oakland are also being funded by the Department of Transportation. The studies and tests are no doubt necessary. But immediate action is called for as well.

Volpe has approved the idea of creating a mass transit "trust fund." Such a plan would allocate certain tax moneys directly to mass transit improvement programs. He has said that some cost sharing will be necessary. That is, the cities will provide a certain share of the money and the federal government will supply the rest, the federal contribution being greater than that of the individual city. Perhaps some form of tax incentive can also be worked out to induce private firms to involve themselves in mass transit experimentation. Money is needed, and action is needed, and both are needed quickly.

While greater attention will be focused on mass transit in the 1970's, road building will continue at full speed. Indeed, indications are that highway construction may move even faster under Volpe than it did under his predecessor, Alan Boyd, even though most of the transportation expenditures in previous budgets went toward highway building. In 1967, for example, highways claimed 90 per cent of urban transportation appropriations funds, with public transit picking up the remaining 10 per cent. And that is only for urban transportation. Including interstate and nonurban highway construction, the relationship was even more lopsided. The balance must be righted. If our mass transit systems are to advance into the modern era, if they are to utilize the technological resources that we now have available, and if they are to serve the communities and their surroundings, then great expenditures will be necessary.

Some of the transportation systems that have been proposed for the future are highly intriguing. They draw upon sophisticated techniques that at present are employed only in building weapons or rockets to the moon. They call for cars skimming over a track that billows air, creating a sort of suction effect; elaborate monorail systems to travel at high speeds through our large cities; small individual vehicles to carry commuters to work from their suburban homes, with computers assuring minimal delays and constant availability of cars. By comparison, our present systems resemble glorified stagecoaches—which, in a very real sense, they are.

One proposed plan would combine present-day systems with the futuristic systems mentioned above. The "Dial-a-Bus" would combine ordinary buses and ordinary roads with some advanced communications equipment to achieve a greatly improved bus system, with door-to-door routes and no delays. It would work as a combined bus-taxi. The potential passenger would call the central command post, state his address, his destination, and the time he wished to go. The computerized command post would then direct one of the buses in the vicinity to pick up the passenger and deliver him to where he wanted to go. This system would be particularly valuable in areas with low population densities, such as outlying suburban communities. The advantages would be brief waiting time and door-to-door service. It would be similar to the shared taxis that are becoming common at big city airports, but it could charge far less than taxis. It need not be too costly to test such a system. The HUD report suggests that a limited demonstration of its effectiveness could be made in less than three years at a cost of a million dollars, or on a more elaborate plane, a full-scale demonstration could be made in seven years for less than $20 million.[13] Such a system, of course, would be little more than a vastly more efficient bus system, plus the advantages of the more personalized taxi. There is no reason why "Dial-a-Bus" could not be instituted, with conventional means of public transportation—buses and subways—still in use where the demand warranted.

"Transportation," Alan Boyd wrote recently, "is only one facet of the total problem, only one element of any potential cure. But it is a pervasive element, touching on all the others."[14] If our cities are to be liveable and workable in the years ahead, we must attack the problems of public transportation. If we are to enjoy clean air, we must make our transportation systems pollution-free. In the future, as more and more stationary sources of pollution are brought under control, a gigantic task in itself requiring massive amounts of money and effort, the air will still be poisonous if we do not clean up our transportation systems.

It is now apparent that our air pollution and our transportation problems are not being adequately faced. Innovation does not seem to come easily in our society. As Richard Morse has pointed out, most new products have been developed by companies or individuals outside of the particular industry producing the product being replaced. Synthetic fibers were first invented by people removed from the wool and cotton industry. The copying machine was invented by people outside of the office machinery industry. The Polaroid camera was not developed by the photographic industry. It seems clear now that improvements in transportation will not come from the railroad or automotive industries. One does not have the capability, and the other does not have the interest.

Right now, steam cars are being tested, and their effectiveness in cleaning up our contaminated air will receive practical demonstration. Hopefully, we will soon be able to buy steam-powered automobiles—and buy them we must if we are to have a clean environment in the years ahead.

Notes

One The Poisoned Air

1 *Waste Management and Control*, a report of the National Academy of Sciences, referred to in "Pollution: Causes, Costs, Controls," *Chemical and Engineering News*, June 9, 1969.
2 Dr. A. J. Haagen-Smit, chairman of the California Air Resources Board, quoted in Philip M. Boffey, "Smog: Los Angeles Running Hard, Standing Still," *Science*, Volume 161, September 6, 1968, p. 991.
3 Howard Lewis, *With Every Breath You Take* (New York, Crown Publishers, 1965), has discussion of temperature inversions, pp. 30–36.
4 Unidentified Doctor (Doctor X), Donora, Pennsylvania, quoted in "A Breath of Death: The Fatality Factor of Smog," a transcript of a special report by Al Wiman broadcast on KLAC radio, Los Angeles, October 1967, p. 6.

5 Albert Delsandro, quoted in Wiman, p. 7.

6 An interesting explanation of Dr. Greenburg's research techniques is given in Edward Edelson and Fred Warshofsky, *Poisons in the Air* (New York, Pocket Books, 1966), pp. 19–24.

7 John Lindsay, addressing the annual meeting of the National Air Pollution Control Association, June 24, 1969, quoted in David Bird, "Air Gets Cleaner, Lindsay Contends," *The New York Times*, June 25, 1969, p. 34.

8 "Rationale for Air Quality Criteria," based on a staff report prepared by Fred Grundy for the subcommittee on air and water pollution of the Senate Public Works Committee, July 1968. Printed in *Environmental Science and Technology*, October 1968, p. 742.

9 This photochemical result is the technical definition of *smog*. However, the word, a combination of *smoke* and *fog*, has been used for decades to refer to all types of air pollution. Only London and Los Angeles air pollution are described as "smog" in this chapter.

10 Dr. John R. Goldsmith and Dr. Stephen A. Landaw, "Carbon Monoxide and Human Health," *Science*, Volume 162, December 20, 1968, p. 1358.

11 Ibid., p. 1356.

12 Lewis, in Chapter 8, describes the unhealthy effects of carbon monoxide. Donald Carr, *The Breath of Life* (New York, W. W. Norton, 1965) discusses carbon monoxide in Chapter 4. Both books also deal with the effects of other pollutants on health.

13 Edith Iglauer, "Reporter at Large: The Ambient Air," *The New Yorker*, April 13, 1968, p. 69.

14 *The Automobile and Air Pollution: A Program for Progress*, a report of the panel on electrically-powered vehicles, Department of Commerce, Part I, October 1967, p. 24.

15 Dr. Robert Horton, director of the Health Effects Research Program, Cincinnati, Ohio, quoted in Iglauer, p. 113.

16 Dr. Kay H. Jones, assistant to the associate director for control technology research and development, National Center for Air Pollution Control, Department of Health, Education, and Welfare, interview, November 25, 1968.

17 Dr. Seymour Calvert, director of California Air Pollution Research Center, University of California at Riverside, testimony at hearings of HEW, San Francisco, January 15, 1968.

18 Dr. H. Richard Weinerman, professor of medicine and public health, Yale University, at panel discussion on automobiles

at Yale, December 1, 1968, quoted in "Auto Called No. 1 Health Enemy," *The New York Times*, December 2, 1968.

Two Detroit's Reaction

1 Dr. John T. Middleton and Dr. Wayne Ott, "Air Pollution and Transportation," *Traffic Quarterly*, July 1968, p. 181.
2 Kenneth Hahn, quoted in "A Breath of Death: The Fatality Factor of Smog," a transcript of a special report by Al Wiman broadcast on KLAC radio, Los Angeles, October 1967, p. 9.
3 The phrase is Ralph Nader's, from *Unsafe At Any Speed* (New York, Pocket Books, 1966), p. 120.
4 Resolution 180 of the County of Los Angeles Board of Supervisors, 1965, reprinted as Appendix B in Nader, p. 265.
5 In the long run, carbon dioxide could be dangerous if too much of it gets into the atmosphere. From Howard Lewis, *With Every Breath You Take* (New York, Crown, 1965): "Carbon dioxide in the atmosphere lets the sun's radiations through to strike the earth's surface. But, like the glass roof of a greenhouse, the carbon dioxide prevents the resulting heat from escaping. The end effect is that the earth is warming up" (p. 130). The long-range result of this so-called "greenhouse effect" will be warmer temperatures throughout the earth, causing the polar ice caps to melt and many life forms to be destroyed. In the short term, however, for about the next couple of hundred years, this should not be too much of a problem.
6 Dr. Kay H. Jones, assistant to the associate director for control technology research and development, National Center for Air Pollution Control, Department of Health, Education, and Welfare, interview, November 25, 1968.
7 S. Smith Griswold, "Regulation of New Motor Vehicles," presented at second plenary session of the National Conference on Air Pollution, Washington, D. C., December 13, 1966.
8 Charles Heinen, quoted in Wiman, p. 34.
9 Ibid., p. 35.
10 *The Automobile and Air Pollution: A Program for Progress*, a report of the panel on electrically-powered vehicles, Department of Commerce, Part II, December 1967, p. 3. Lewis, op. cit., also discusses the effects of nitrogen oxides on health at various places in his book.
11 Griswold.
12 Middleton and Ott, pp. 181–182.

13 Miles L. Brubacher and J. C. Raymond, "California Vehicle Exhaust Control—Past and Future," presented at annual meeting of the Air Pollution Control Association, St. Paul, Minnesota, June 27, 1968.

14 Ibid.

15 Ibid.

16 Robert Barsky, deputy air pollution control officer of the Los Angeles Air Pollution Control District, strongly concurs with Maga. Quoted in Jerry M. Flint, "Auto Man Claims Victory on Fumes," *The New York Times*, April 13, 1969, Barsky said that since especially tuned models are used in testing emissions, the auto companies have "not achieved the goals, which were inadequate anyway. When you start out with a faulty premise you come out with a faulty conclusion."

17 "Pollution: Causes, Costs, Controls," *Chemical and Engineering News*, June 9, 1969, p. 38.

18 Dr. A. J. Haagen-Smit, private correspondence, November 22, 1968.

19 John R. Goldsmith in a letter to *Science*, volume 163, p. 1010. The letter was in answer to correspondence concerning an article that he wrote in collaboration with Stephen A. Landaw, "Carbon Monoxide and Human Health," *Science*, volume 162, p. 1352 (December 20, 1968).

20 Henry Ford II, quoted in "An Informal Visit With Henry Ford," *Look*, May 28, 1968.

21 William P. Lear, interview, December 19, 1968.

Three   The Steam Car Historically

1 Anthony Bird, *The Motor Car: 1765–1914* (B. T. Batsford, Ltd., London, 1960), p. 17.

2 "Steam Automobiles," *Literary Digest*, July 5, 1919, quoting article that appeared in *The Universal Engineer*, May 1919.

3 Bird, p. 21.

4 Hiram Percy Maxim, *Horseless Carriage Days* (Harper and Brothers, New York, 1937), quoted in Bird, p. 168, 171.

5 F. E. Stanley, quoted in M. M. Musselman, *Get A Horse* (J. B. Lippincott, Philadelphia, 1950), p. 92.

6 John Carlova, "The Stanleys and Their Steamer," *American Heritage*, February 1959.

7 Stanley in Musselman, p. 98. The speed of the car has been questioned, however. Dr. Robert U. Ayres, vice-president of International Research and Technology, Washington, D. C., says that the 197 mph is a "widespread rumor, but apparently

untrue." He says that "it was probably impossible for the Stanley engine to go that fast. What *did* happen was that the car hit a bump and 'took off.'"

8 J. D. Nies, "Figures on the Steam Car," letter to the editor of *Scientific American*, November 25, 1916.

9 Hugh G. Boutell, "A Word for the Steam Automobile," letter to the editor of *Scientific American*, July 31, 1920.

10 W. J. Parrish, "The Steam Car Again," letter to the editor of *Scientific American*, November 8, 1919.

11 E. T. Adams, "Steam Engines in the Automotive Field," presented at annual meeting of the American Society of Mechanical Engineers, and printed in the *Journal of the Society of Automotive Engineers*. Reprinted in the *Scientific American Supplement*, October 5, 1918.

12 "New Type of Steam Motor Car," *Scientific American*, December 23, 1916.

13 "Will the Steam Automobile Return?" *Scientific American*, January 1928.

Four The Steam Car Today

1 "Autos: Voltswagen," *Newsweek*, September 26, 1966. J. F. Barnes and K. W. Bennett, "Watts Happening in Autos," *The Iron Age*, October 13, 1966. "Welcome Back, Electrics," *The Evening Star* (Washington, D. C.), September 21, 1966. James Ridgeway, "Back to Electric Cars?" *The New Republic*, August 13, 1966. "1960 Shapes Up as Key Year for Renaissance of the Electric Vehicle," *Electrical World*, January 18, 1960.

2 J. Herbert Hollomon, testimony on "Electric Vehicles and Other Alternatives to the Internal Combustion Engine," at joint hearings of the Senate Commerce Committee and Public Works Committee's subcommittee on air and water pollution, Washington, D. C., April 10, 1967. (In printed copy of the hearings, p. 396.)

3 *The Automobile and Air Pollution: A Program for Progress*, a report of the panel on electrically-powered vehicles, Department of Commerce, Part I, October 1967, p. 7.

4 Ibid., Part II, December 1967, p. 61.

5 "Steam—The Answer to Smog?" written by the staff of *Road Test*, special steam car issue, *Road Test*, December 1967.

6 Ibid.

7 Donald Johnson, quoted in Andrew Jamison, "Steam Cars: Jet Tycoon, Others, Espouse the Cause," *Science*, Vol. 163, January 24, 1969, p. 374.

8 S. William Gouse, "For Smog's Sake, Steam-Powered Automobiles Should Come Back," *Engineer*, May—June 1968.

Five The Steam People

1 Letter from William P. Lear to James B. Rogers, Jr., Rich-
   mond, Virginia, November 1, 1968.
2 Ibid.
3 Richard Morse, "A Suggested Program for Government and
   Industry in Solving the Automotive Emissions Problem," paper presented at annual meeting of the Society of Automotive
   Engineers, January 1968.

Six Lear

1 William P. Lear, quoted in Andrew Jamison, "Steam Cars:
   Jet Tycoon, Others, Espouse the Cause," *Science*, Volume
   163, January 24, 1969, p. 370.
2 William P. Lear in Bob Ottum, "Let There Be Steam," *Sports
   Illustrated*, February 3, 1969, p. 53.
3 Letter from William P. Lear to James B. Rogers, Jr., Rich-
   mond, Virginia, November 1, 1968.
4 Lear in Ottum.
5 Lear letter.
6 Ibid.
7 Dick Wells, "Lear's Steam Dream: A Reality?" *Motor Trend*,
   June 1969, p. 27.
8 Lear letter.
9 Lear in Ottum, p. 53.
10 Lear letter.
11 William P. Lear, quoted in William Trombley, "Lear Pre-
   dicts Success for His New Steam Automobile," *The Los Angeles Times*, November 9, 1968.

Seven California's Activity

1 Arthur Bolton, "Expanding the Power of State Legislatures,"
   paper presented at State Legislator's Seminar, Key Biscayne,
   Florida, July 1968.
2 Ibid.
3 Ibid.
4 Carlos Bee, "Research in the Legislature," paper presented at
   the meeting of the Western Government Research Association, Lake Tahoe, Nevada, October 26, 1967.

5 Memorandum to the California Assembly Committee on Transportation and Commerce from Karsten J. Vieg, October 5, 1967.

6 Ibid.

7 Ibid.

8 Statement of Assemblyman John F. Foran in presenting Assembly Bill 357 on the floor of California State Assembly, April 1968.

9 "Report to the Assembly Committee on Transportation and Commerce," from the Technical Advisory Panel on the Pure Air Act of 1968 (AB 357), April 14, 1968, p. 16.

10 William Lipman, interview in *IDEAS* (Information on Developments in Electricity and Steam), Vol. 1, November 1968, p. 13.

11 Private correspondence from Arie J. Haagen-Smit, November 22, 1968.

12 Letter from H. W. Sullivan to Assemblyman John F. Foran, March 22, 1968.

13 R. A. Kridler, quoted in Highway Patrol press release, October 10, 1968.

14 Letter from H. W. Sullivan to steam engine makers, October 28, 1968.

15 Original "Request for Proposals" for California Highway Patrol steam-car testing program, sent to prospective bidders, August 1968.

16 Lipman.

17 John F. Foran, quoted in "Patrol May Try Out Steam Cars," Sacramento *Bee*, May 21, 1968.

18 Lipman, pp. 13–14.

19 See John Lear, "Green Light for the Smogless Car," *Saturday Review*, December 6, 1969, pp. 81–86, for details on the bus program, as well as background on William Brobeck's company.

20 Jim Roth, quoted in "Dallas To Test Freon Bus Engine," *The New York Times*, February 24, 1969.

Eight The Role of the Federal Government

1 "Progress in the Prevention and Control of Air Pollution," first report of the Secretary of Health, Education, and Welfare to the Congress of the United States in compliance with Public Law 90-148, May 1968, p. i.

2 S. Smith Griswold, testimony at hearings before a special subcommittee on air and water pollution of the Senate Public

Works Committee on Air Pollution Control, Washington, D. C., September 9–11, 1963. (In printed copy of hearings, p. 141.)

3 HEW report, pp. i–ii.

4 Kay H. Jones, assistant to the associate commissioner for control technology research and development, National Center for Air Pollution Control, HEW, interview, November 25, 1968.

5 HEW report, p. iii.

6 Bryce Nelson, "Air Quality Act of 1967: A Step Forward, But Don't Expect Immediate Improvement of Your Air," *Science*, Vol. 158, October 20, 1967, p. 355.

7 Senator Warren Magnuson, statement at joint hearings of the Senate Commerce Committee and Public Works Committee's subcommittee on air and water pollution on "Electric Vehicles and Other Alternatives to the Internal Combustion Engine," Washington, D. C., March 14, 1967. (In printed copy of hearings, p. 1.)

8 Lawrence Lessing, "The Revolt Against the Internal-Combustion Engine," *Fortune*, July 1967, p. 184.

9 Alan Boyd, testimony at electric car hearings. (In printed copy of hearings, p. 69.)

10 Stewart Udall, testimony at electric car hearings, March 17, 1967. (In printed copy of hearings, p. 311.)

11 Senator Philip Hart, statement at electric car hearings, March 14, 1967. (In printed copy of hearings, p. 104.)

12 Boyd, testimony at electric car hearings. (In printed copy of hearings, p. 87.)

13 Senator Russell Long, statement at electric car hearings, March 15, 1967. (In printed copy of hearings, pp. 187, 188.)

14 *The Automobile and Air Pollution: A Program for Progress*, a report of the panel on electrically-powered vehicles, Department of Commerce, Part I, October 1967, p. 45.

15 Ibid., p. 3.

16 California Assemblyman John F. Foran, statement sent to joint hearings of the Senate Commerce Committee and Public Works Committee's subcommittee on air and water pollution on "Automobile Steam Engine and Other External Combustion Engines," Washington, D.C., May 27–28, 1968. (Reprinted in printed copy of hearings, pp. 173–174.)

17 Magnuson, quoted in Morton Mintz, "Bills Aim to Spur Low-Pollution Cars," *The Washington Post*, November 27, 1969, p. 2.

18 Ibid.

Nine The Other Alternatives

1 Michael Ference, statement at joint hearings of the Senate Commerce Committee and Public Works Committee's subcommittee on air and water pollution on "Electric Vehicles and Other Alternatives to the Internal Combustion Engine," Washington, D. C., March 16, 1967. (In printed copy of hearings, p. 223.)

2 Horace Heyman, testimony at electric car hearings, op. cit., March 15, 1967. (In printed copy of hearings, p. 165.)

3 Lloyd Orr, statement at hearings before the subcommittee on Antitrust and Monopoly of the Senate Judiciary Committee on "Economic Concentration: Part 6, New Technologies and Concentration," Washington, D. C., September 26, 1967. (In printed copy of hearings, p. 2787.)

4 John Radosta, "New Electric Car Can Revolutionize Travel in Future," *The New York Times*, December 1, 1968.

5 Ference.

6 *The Automobile and Air Pollution: A Program for Progress*, a report of the panel on electrically-powered vehicles, Department of Commerce, Part II, December 1967, p. 67.

7 Henry Ford II, quoted in "An Informal Visit With Henry Ford," *Look*, May 28, 1968.

8 Jacob Goldman, quoted in "Ford Electric Car Crisis," *Motor Trend*, March 1969, p. 11.

9 *The Automobile and Air Pollution*, op. cit., Part II, p. 73.

10 Robert Ayres, "Alternative Nonpolluting Power Sources," *Society of Automotive Engineers Journal*, Vol. 76, December 1968, p. 52.

11 *The Automobile and Air Pollution*, Part I, October 1967, p. 2.

12 American Society of Mechanical Engineers citation, as quoted in Julian G. Schmidt, "Here Come Th' Judge," *Motor Trend*, January 1969, p. 30.

13 George Huebner, quoted in Schmidt.

14 Ford Motor Company statement, presented to the California Assembly Committee on Transportation and Commerce, December 7, 1967, Sacramento, California.

15 J. A. Hoess, et. al. (of the Battelle Memorial Institute), "Summary Report on Study of Unconventional Thermal, Mechanical, and Nuclear Low-Pollution-Potential Power Sources for Urban Vehicles," for the National Center for Air Pollution Control, Department of Health, Education, and Welfare, March 15, 1968, p. 39.

16 *The Automobile and Air Pollution*, Part II, pp. 58, 60.

17 Robert Thompson, technical director for engineering research
    for General Motors Research Laboratories, quoted in
    Schmidt, p. 33.
18 *The Automobile and Air Pollution*, Part II, p. 58.

Ten   Some Conclusions

1 Frank Stead, quoted in testimony of Alex Radin, general man-
    ager of the American Public Power Association, at joint
    hearings of Senate Commerce Committee and Public Works
    Committee's subcommittee on air and water pollution on
    "Electric Vehicles and Other Alternatives to the Internal
    Combustion Engine," Washington, D. C., March 15, 1967.
    (In printed copy of hearings, p. 143.)
 2 Yule Fisher, director of the National Highway Users Confer-
    ence Inc., "Highway Proponent," letter sent to the editor of
    The Wall Street Journal, March 19, 1969.
 3 John Volpe, quoted in Joseph Sullivan, "City Curbs on Autos
    Seen," *Newark Evening News*, March 10, 1969.
 4 Volpe, quoted in Ken Hartnett, "Transit Only Hope For
    Cities—Volpe," *Boston Evening Globe*, March 26, 1969.
 5 *Tomorrow's Transportation*, Department of Housing and Ur-
    ban Development, May 1968, p. 8.
 6 Ibid., p. 9.
 7 Volpe, quoted in Hartnett.
 8 Ibid.
 9 *Tomorrow's Transportation*, p. 11.
10 Ibid.
11 Ibid., p. 17.
12 Ibid., pp. 44 ff.
13 Ibid., p. 60.
14 Alan Boyd, "Slow Motion," *Business Today*, Spring 1969,
    pp. 19–20.

Index

Adams, E. T., 47–48
American Motors, 17, 92
Arthur D. Little, Inc., 58
Automobile Manufacturers Association, 17
Ayres, Robert U., 56–59, 62–64, 71–72, 76, 104, 108, 111–12, 114, 121–22, 137

Baker, Howard, 21–22
Battelle Institute, 58, 125, 139
Bee, Carlos, 101
Besler, George, 31
Besler, William, 72
Black, Robert, 81
Bolton, Arthur, 99–100
Boyd, Alan, 120, 122, 151
Brobeck, William, 112
Brubacher, Miles L., 25

California Air Resources Board, 15, 16, 24–25, 27, 117–18
California Highway Patrol (CHP), steam-car testing program, 76, 78, 79, 91, 94, 107–11, 126
California State Assembly, 98 ff.
Assembly Bill (AB) 356, 104–106, 111
Committee on Transportation and Commerce, 1967 pollution hearings, 102–103, 139; steam-car hearings (1968), 58, 71, 105–107
Office of Research, 99, 100–101
Pure Air Act (AB 357), 103–105
Chrysler Motors Corp., 17, 23, 71, 137–39

Connor, John T., 54
Coston, Dean W., 120
Cugnot, Nicholas J., 36–37, 41
Curran, Frank, 48, 50, 51

Doble, Abner, 46, 47, 48–50, 52, 65, 72, 74, 112
Dooley, James, 112

Electric cars, 52–53, 55–56, 58, 129–136. *See also* U.S. Senate electric car hearings.
Electric Fuel Propulsion, Inc., 133
Empirical Engineering Co., 95
Energy Systems, Inc., 55, 80–82

Ference, Michael, 131–32, 134
Finch, Robert, 118
Foley, Thomas, 127
Foran, John F., 101, 102, 103, 104, 105, 107, 111, 126
Ford, Henry, 43, 49, 85, 131
Ford, Henry, II, 30–31, 135
Ford Motor Co., 17, 21, 30–31, 33, 53, 60, 75, 125, 135–36, 137, 138, 139
Foster, Berry, 109
Fuller, Louis J., 4, 102

Galvin, Paul, 87
Gardner, John, 117, 143
General Motors Corp., 17, 31, 53, 60, 76, 82, 108, 110, 135, 137, 140
General Steam Corp., 63, 66, 76–79, 83, 109–110, 112
Gibbs, R. A., 59, 72, 73
Goldman, Jacob, 136
Goldsmith, John, 29
Gouse, S. William, 64–65, 66–67, 112
Granatelli, Andy, 90, 125, 137
Greenburg, Leonard, 6
Griswold, S. Smith, 4, 23–24, 116

Haagen-Smit, A. J., 14–15, 29, 105
Hafstad, Lawrence, 31, 32
Hahn, Kenneth, 15

Hart, Philip, 120
Hatsopoulos, George, 73
Heinen, Charles, 23
Heyman, Horace, 131–32
Hollomon, J. Herbert, 53–54, 120
Hosick, Thomas, 60, 72
Huebner, George, 138
Hughes, Howard, 108

International Research and Technology, 56

Jackson, Henry, 127
James, W. H., 37
Johnson, Donald, 63, 66–67, 76–79, 84, 109
Johnson, Theodore, 32, 73, 75
Jones, Kay, 125–26

Kaye, Joseph, 73
Keen, Charles, 72
Kridler, R. A., 109

Lane Steamer, 45
Lanterman, Frank, 108
Lear Motors Corp., *see* Lear, William P.
Lear, William P., 65, 67, 72, 76, 85–97, 109, 110, 111, 112
Leuthje, D. S., 109–10
Lindsay, John, 7, 128
Ling-Temco-Vought, Inc. (LTV), 108–109, 112–13, 125
Lipman, William, 104–107, 110–11, 126
Long, Russell, 122
Los Angeles Air Pollution Control District (APCD), 4–5, 15, 102, 116
Lyons, Robert, 70, 106

Maga, John, 25–29, 61, 105, 112
Magnuson, Warren, 118–119, 121, 127–28
Marriott, Fred, 44
Maxim, Hiram P., 39–40
McCloskey, Paul, 127
McCulloch Motors, 50, 52, 112
McCulloch, Robert Paxton, *see* McCulloch Motors

Middleton, John, 14, 18, 24, 125–26

Miner, Samuel, 106, 112

Minto, Wallace, 75–76, 109, 112–13

Misch, Herbert, 21–22, 30, 33

Mobil Oil Co., 33, 80

Morse panel, *see* Morse, Richard, *and* U.S. Dept. of Commerce Panel on Electrically-Powered Vehicles

Morse, Richard, 53–56, 59, 64, 66, 67, 79–83, 85, 126–27, 151

Moulton, Alex, 50

Muskie, Edmund, 118–19, 121, 127

Nadar, Ralph, 121, 133

National Center for Air Pollution Control, *see* U.S. Dept. of Health, Education, and Welfare

Newcomen, Thomas, 36

Orr, Lloyd D., 123–24, 132–33

Ottinger, Richard, 143–44

Paxton, Douglas, 112

Paxton steam car, 50

Paxve, Inc., 112

Pearson, James, 32

Peterson, Karl, 95, 106, 109

Peugeot, Armand, 40

Ragone, David, 55

Raymond, J. C., 25

Reid, Joan, 101

Scientific Analysis Corp. (SAC), 111–12

Serpollet, Leon, 40, 42, 84, 85

Smith, R. G., 76–79, 83

Smith, Richard, 95, 106, 109

Society of Automotive Engineers (SAE), 79–80

Stanley, F. E., and F. O., *see* Stanley Steamer

Stanley Steamer, 41–45, 50–51, 60, 65, 84–85

Stead, Frank, 143

Steam Automobile Club, 57, 70, 106, 112

Steam Power Systems, Inc., 90, 112

Stirling engine, 57

Sullivan, H. W., 107, 109

Thermal Kinetics Corp., 72

Thermodynamics Systems, Inc., 78

Thermo Electron Corp., 31–32, 59, 66, 73–75, 76, 125

Trevithick, Richard, 36–37, 41

Udall, Stewart, 120

Unruh, Jesse M., 99–100

U.S. Department of Commerce Panel on Electrically-Powered Vehicles (Morse Panel), 12, 53–56, 58, 120–21, 124–25, 135–38, 140

U.S. Department of Health, Education, and Welfare (HEW), National Center for Air Pollution Control, 23, 32, 58, 75, 118, 125–26, 139

U.S. Department of Housing and Urban Development (HUD), 80–82, 118; report, "Tomorrow's Transportation," 146–48, 150

U.S. Department of Transportation (DOT), steam-bus testing program, 76, 81, 90, 111–13, 126, 149; Secretaries of Transportation, 120, 145

U.S. Senate Commerce Committee, 118; staff report (1969), 123, 127; steam-car hearings held jointly with Public Works Committee's Subcommittee on Air and Water Pollution (May 1968), 21–22, 31–34, 59–61, 63, 64, 70–71, 73, 106, 114, 121–24, 127, 143–44

U.S. Senate Public Works Committee, Subcommittee on Air and Water Pollution, 8, 116, 118; electric car hearings (March 1967), 119–21, 122,

131–32; steam-car hearings, *see* U.S. Senate Commerce Committee, steam-car hearings (May 1968).

Vieg, Karsten, 70, 71, 91, 101–109, 111, 126
Volpe, John, 145–49

Wallis, Ken, 90–91, 112
Watt, James, 36
White, Rollin, *see* White Steamer
White Steamer, 44–46, 73, 85
Williams, Calvin and Charles, 33–34, 59–60, 65, 69–72, 74, 80, 84, 85, 104, 106–107, 108, 109